CRAZY
BRAVE

W. W. NORTON & COMPANY | New York · London

CRAZY
BRAVE

A

MEMOIR

JOY HARJO

For information about permission to reproduce selections from this book,
write to Permissions, W. W. Norton & Company, Inc.,
500 Fifth Avenue, New York, NY 10110

For information about special discounts for bulk purchases, please contact
W. W. Norton Special Sales at specialsales@wwnorton.com or 800-233-4830

Manufacturing by Courier Westford
Book design by JAMdesign
Production manager: Julia Druskin

Library of Congress Cataloging-in-Publication Data

Harjo, Joy.
Crazy brave : a memoir / Joy Harjo. — 1st ed.
p. cm.
ISBN 978-0-393-07346-1 (hardcover)
1. Harjo, Joy. 2. Women poets, American—Biography.
3. Indian authors—United States—Biography. I. Title.
PS3558.A62423Z46 2012
811'.54—dc23
[B]
2012011198

W. W. Norton & Company, Inc.
500 Fifth Avenue, New York, N.Y. 10110
www.wwnorton.com

W. W. Norton & Company Ltd.
Castle House, 75/76 Wells Street, London W1T 3QT

1 2 3 4 5 6 7 8 9 0

To the warriors of the heart
To my teachers in the
East, North, West, and South,
Above and Below

CONTENTS

Once I traveled far above the earth. This beloved planet we call home was covered with an elastic web of light. I watched in awe as it shimmered, stretched, dimmed, and shined, shaped by the collective effort of all life within it. Dissonance attracted more dissonance. Harmony attracted harmony. I saw revolutions, droughts, famines, and the births of new nations. The most humble kindnesses made the brightest lights. Nothing was wasted.

CRAZY BRAVE

EAST

East is the direction of beginnings. It is sunrise. When beloved Sun rises, it is an entrance, a door to fresh knowledge. Breathe the light in. Call upon the assistance you need for the day. Give thanks.

East is how the plants, animals, and other beings orient themselves for beginnings, to open and blossom. The spirit of the day emerges from the sunrise point. East is also the direction of Oklahoma, where I was born, the direction of the Creek Nation.

nce I was so small I could barely see over the top of the back seat of the black Cadillac my father bought with his Indian oil money. He polished and tuned his car daily. I wanted to see everything.

This was around the time I acquired language, when something happened that changed my relationship to the spin of the world. It changed even the way I looked at the sun.

This suspended integer of time probably escaped ordinary notice in my parents' universe, which informed most of my vision in the ordinary world. They were still omnipresent gods.

We were driving somewhere in Tulsa, the northern border of the Creek Nation. I don't know where we were going or where we had been, but I know the sun was boiling the asphalt, the car windows were open for any breeze as I stood on tiptoes on the floorboard behind my father, a handsome god who smelled of Old Spice, whose slick black hair was always impeccably groomed, his clothes perfectly creased and ironed. The radio was on. Even then I loved the radio, jukeboxes, or any magic thing containing music.

I wonder what signaled this moment, a loop of time that on first glance could be any place in time. I became acutely aware of the line the jazz trumpeter was playing (a sound I later associated with Miles Davis). I didn't know the words *jazz* or *trumpet*. I don't know how to say it, with what sounds or words, but in that confluence of hot southern afternoon, in the breeze of aftershave and humidity, I followed that sound to the beginning, to the birth of sound. I was suspended in whirling stars. I grieved my parents' failings, my own life, which I saw stretching the length of that rhapsody.

My rite of passage into the world of humanity occurred then, through jazz. The music was a startling bridge between familiar and strange lands. I heard stomp-dance shells, singing. I saw suits, satin, fine hats. I heard workers singing in the fields. It was a way to speak beyond the confines of ordinary language.

I still hear it.

> —Over and over and over.
> When you gonna come back, baby?
> —Over and over and over.
> Why did you leave me?
> The god of all things reached
> Behind the counter, pulled up a sour dishrag and
> Cleaned off the mess.
> —We all went tumbling down.
> I said, over and over and over.
> —We all went tumbling down.

My mother's singing attracted me to her road in this world. It is her song that lit my attention as I listened in the ancestor realm. Secret longing rose up in her heart as she sang along with the radio. The music threading the atmosphere in what was known as Tulsa, Oklahoma, or "T-Town," in 1951 was songs for falling in love, songs for falling out of love, songs to endure the purgatory of longing, or improvisational swing jazz, country, or songs just for the sake of kicking it.

Tulsa was a Creek Indian town established on the Arkansas River, after my father's people were forcibly removed from their homes in the South in the mid-1800s. When they arrived in these new lands, they brought sacred fire. They brought what they could carry. Some African people came with them as family members, others as slaves. Other African people arrived independently, established their own towns. European and American settlers soon took over the lands that were established for settlement of eastern tribes in what became known as Indian Territory. The Christian god gave them authority. Yet everyone wanted the same thing: land, peace, a place to make a home, cook, fall in love, make children and music.

Every soul has a distinct song. Even the place called Tulsa has a song that rises up from the Arkansas River around sundown.

I heard the soul that was to be my mother call out in a heartbreak ballad. I saw her walking the floor after midnight. Though she was crazy in love with my father, she sensed the hard road ahead of them. I heard Cherokee stomp dancers in the distance. They were her mother's people. They danced under the stars until the light of dawn. I saw a young Irishman cross over waters, forced by politics and poverty. He married into the Cherokee people. He is one of her ancestors. Over in the east I saw a hill above the river. There was my mother's dream house. She had four children, two boys and two girls. Everyone had a bed and shoes. No one ever went hungry.

Because music is a language that lives in the spiritual realms, we can hear it, we can notate it and create it, but we cannot hold it in our hands. Music can help raise a people up or call them to gather for war. The song my mother-to-be was singing will make my father love her, forever, but it will not keep him out of the arms of other women. I will find my way to earth by her voice.

▲   ▲   ▲

Though I was reluctant to be born, I was attracted by the music. I had plans. I was entrusted with carrying voices, songs, and stories to grow and release into the world, to be of assistance and inspiration. These were my responsibility. I am not special. It is this way for everyone. We enter into a family story, and then other stories based on tribal clans, on tribal towns and nations, lands, countries, planetary systems, and universes. Yet we each have our own individual soul story to tend.

As I approached the doorway to Earth, I was hesitant to enter. I kept looking over my shoulder. I heard the crisp voice of the releaser of souls urge me forward.

"Don't look back!"

And I remembered how Earth is a heavy teacher yet is so much loved by the creator of planetary beings. I did not want to leave mystery, yet I was ever curious and ready to take my place in the story.

My mother wanted a baby to show her love for her husband, my father.

My father didn't know what he wanted. If he was going to have a child, he preferred a son, though in his everyday world in the racist Oklahoma of the fifties, it was difficult for an Indian man, especially one who had no living Indian father or grandfather to show him the way. Most people on my father's side of the family passed from this place relatively young. I am one of the oldest living relatives of our family line. My generation is now the door to memory. This is why I am remembering.

My father was born of tribal leadership. Monahwee, who was one of the leaders of the Red Stick War, which culminated in the Battle of Horseshoe Bend, the largest Indian uprising in the country, was his grandfather, six generations back on his mother's side. Monahwee is still a beloved person to the Creek, or Mvskoke people. Samuel Checotah, another grandfather, was the first principal chief after we settled in Indian Territory, or Oklahoma. Osceola, the Seminole warrior who refused to sign a treaty with the United States government, was our uncle.

As I write this I hear the din of voices of so many people, and so many stories that want to come forth. Each name is a tributary to many others, to many places. I see the spirit of New Orleans and hear the singing of the spirit of Congo Square. Congo Square was originally a southeastern Indian ceremonial ground. It became a meeting place for tribal peoples, Africans, and their European friends, lovers, and families. They gathered there to dance, to enjoy the music and the food wrapped in cloths and gourds they brought to share. This was the place of gossip, news, philosophy, and history. These people, our ancestors, want to be recognized; they want to be remembered.

I see Osceola's mother, Polly Coppinger, as she stands there with her hands on her hips and a reddish glint to her black, heavy, kinky hair. She was born during times of great transition for the Mvskoke Nation. She was charismatic, with a decided stubbornness, and passed this on to her son. I have seen her African ancestors often in my dreams. They gave me a doorway in a dream one night when I was in my very early thirties. It was a waking dream. I was in a village in West Africa. It was another time. I was wrapped in a mat after fasting for several days. I was carried through several realms and saw many things. I was gone for weeks. Yet I returned the next morning as a young woman with two children living in an apartment in Santa Fe. Some things I remember and some things continue to be kept from me.

My father's grandfather was Henry Marcy Harjo, a man in good standing with the Mvskoke community. He was of the Eufaula Canadian tribal town and became a Baptist pastor with a ministry among the Seminole in Florida. He was a transitional principal chief for one day in the early 1900s. He and my grandmother Katie Monahwee even owned a plantation in Stuart, Florida, and traveled there with the children every winter. The plantation was a large tract of land for farming. The land had been used for growing pineapple. My grandfather didn't like pineapple and had every one of the plants dug up.

His wealth came from the family's allotted lands in Indian Territory. In November 1905, before Indian Territory became the State of Oklahoma, a huge oil gusher was discovered on the allotted lands of Ida E. Glenn. This became known as the Glenn Pool. It was the largest oil field in the Southwest. The family lands were part of this oil find. The family became wealthy. My father's mother, Naomi Harjo, and my aunt Lois Harjo were well educated and received their BFA degrees in art at Oklahoma City University. My aunt Lois Harjo told me that family once owned much of the town of Okmulgee.

My grandmother Naomi died of tuberculosis when my

father was a small child. My father had to cross a gulf of sadness left by her absence to find a place for my mother, and then me and the rest of his children. His mother was unreachable except by memory.

In the end, we must each tend to our own gulfs of sadness, though others can assist us with kindness, food, good words, and music. Our human tendency is to fill these holes with distractions like shopping and fast romance, or with drugs and alcohol.

My father's father, Allen W. Foster, married the caretaker of his children. My father gained stepbrothers and a half-sister. He grew up in a house that became known as the Foster Estate, though it was on his mother's Creek land. When I was growing up, my father received enough in oil royalties to support his love for fine cars. I remember him taking apart and putting back together his black Cadillac and his Ford pickup. When my father passed from this world, the oil royalties were divided among his children. By the mid-eighties my brothers, sister, and I were each receiving about thirty dollars a month. Then the oil company stopped the payments. Stories can be very demanding and need care and assistance. The family oil story has a spirit and it wants my attention.

▲   ▲   ▲

As I continued the journey to enter this realm, I watched my mother and father meet at Casa Loma Dance Hall. My mother was beautiful and magnetic. She was that mix of Cherokee and European that dazzles. She was meticulous in her dress. Her journey to Tulsa took determination on her part. She had to oppose her father, a man who favored her over her six brothers, and set her mother against her. She left her sharecropper family shack with her best friend, Elvira Guerra. They headed to Tulsa with money they made from picking crops.

She set herself to mate for life.

My father was ephemeral. He was about ten percent body. The other ninety percent of him was spirit and it was often unreachable, even to him. This earth can be difficult and jarring. Joy can be known only through despair here.

My father was by nature sensitive. He instinctively understood cloud language, the meanings of birds and their appearances, and water. What took precedence in his expression was his father's violent hand. My father was sent from home at a young age to a military academy. He learned anger as a method to control sensitivity.

When my father asked my mother to dance, she shyly but surely entered his arms. They had just met, yet it felt like they had known each other for as far as forever can reach. When my mother first saw this man who would be my father, she knew he was the one, despite his reputation for being a man who loved women. There were many women chasing after him, buying him drinks, pulling on him to dance. They wanted to touch him for his sensual good looks. I imagine that my mother struck a light inside the deepest room in his heart. His charisma was power that had come down from the ancestors. It is something given to us to use to assist others.

I was close to my father through the end. He never spoke of my mother in a negative manner.

My parents danced. What dancers they were, their feet jumping in swing, together in time.

My mother-to-be was fire. Those of fire move about the earth with inspiration and purpose. They are creative, and can consume and be consumed by their desires. They are looking for purpose, a place in which to create. They can be so entranced with the excitement of creation that their dreams burn up, turn to ashes.

My father-to-be was of the water, and could not find a hold on the banks of earthiness. Water people can easily get lost. And they may not comprehend that they are lost. They succumb easily to the spirits of alcohol and drugs. They will always search for a vision that cannot be found on earth.

Their dance was an ancient dance, one that most of us who take on breath know. It is fate setting the story into place. Within the year, I was born to earth, of water and fire. Because I came through them in this life, I would be quick to despair, and understand how to enter and emerge from ancestor realms. I had no way to translate the journey and what I would find there until I found poetry.

THIS IS MY HEART

This is my heart. It is a good heart.
Weaves a membrane of mist and fire.
When we speak love in the flower world
My heart is close enough to sing to you
in a language too clumsy
for human words.

This is my head. It is a good head.
Whirs inside with a swarm of worries.
What is the source of this mystery?
Why can't I see it right here, right now,
as real as these hands hammering
the world together?

This is my soul. It is a good soul.
It tells me, "Come here, forgetful one."
And we sit together.
We cook a little something to eat,
then a sip of something sweet,
for memory, for memory.

This is my song. It is a good song.
It walked forever the border of fire and water,
climbed ribs of desire to sing to you.
Its new wings quiver with vulnerability.

Come lie next to me.
Put your head here.
My heart is close enough to sing.

Though we have instructions and a map buried in our
hearts when we enter this world, nothing quite prepares us
for the abrupt shift to the breathing realm. Good thoughts
by our parents, relatives, and associations contribute a har-
monious atmosphere to the home and provide great assistance. Disregard and fighting bring difficulty and seed
enmity. Each child has a spirit and its particular relation-

ship to parents, ancestors, and place. The spirit's intent can bring blessings, challenges, or both to the family and to their place in the sea of time.

I have been present at many births—my own, my children's, those of patients in the Santa Fe hospital where I worked as a nursing assistant, and the births of several of my grandchildren.

My first granddaughter, born when I was in my thirties, emerged with her eyes open. She saw through this world into the next. Her eyes fixed on her mother, asking for protection.

Another granddaughter was fierce and determined. Even her hair arranged itself in a fiercely determined manner. Her birth was short, precise, and intense. This granddaughter knows what she wants and bided her time impatiently through babyhood.

When I was born, I put up a fight. I wanted out. The emotional sea of my mother was overwhelming. She and my father were in disagreement. He liked his party, and because she was taking care of a pregnancy she could not go out with him to make sure that he didn't stop anywhere else or forget the path home because of bewitchment by another woman.

I'd seen the map of my life. What lay ahead in the early years was difficult. I wanted a head start, to make my way through as fast as possible. Then, as I got close to the door, I panicked. I began choking and kicking, fighting for air.

My spirit helper spoke precisely: "If you fight water, you drown."

▲   ▲   ▲

On a mountainside in Colorado forty years later, in a vision, I relived my birth. As I struggled through the birth canal, I saw myself as a warrior with a weapon in my hand. I saw the slaughter, a battlefield of fallen comrades. I decided then to take as many enemies with me as possible. I went down, drowning in blood, still fighting. This vision could have been a memory curled in my DNA. The story of my grandfather Monahwee and the people at the Battle of Horseshoe Band was horrific and it made a deep groove in the family and tribal memory.

A story matrix connects all of us.

There are rules, processes, and circles of responsibility in this world. And the story begins exactly where it is supposed to begin. We cannot skip any part.

In some story realms the baby is born and the next day he or she is a giant who kills monsters. Mine was not that kind of story. I am born of brave people and we were in need of warriors. My father and I had lost the way. I was born puny and female and Indian in lands that were stolen. Many of the people were forgetting the songs and stories. Yet others hid out and carried the fire of the songs and stories so we could continue the culture.

In a world long before this one, there was enough for everyone
until somebody got out of line.
We heard it was Rabbit, fooling around with clay and the wind.
Everybody was tired of his tricks and no one would play with
*   him;*
he was lonely in this world.
So Rabbit thought to make a person.

And when he blew into the mouth of that crude figure to see
   what would happen,
the clay man stood up.
Rabbit showed the clay man how to steal a chicken.
The clay man obeyed.
Then Rabbit showed him how to steal corn.
The clay man obeyed.
Then he showed him how to steal someone else's wife.
The clay man obeyed.
Rabbit felt important and powerful.
The clay man felt important and powerful.
And once that clay man started, he could not stop.
Once he took that chicken, he wanted all the chickens.
And once he took that corn, he wanted all the corn.
And once he took that wife, he wanted all the wives.
He was insatiable.
Then he had a taste of gold and he wanted all the gold.
Then it was land and anything else he saw.
His wanting only made him want more.
Soon it was countries, and then it was trade.
The wanting infected the earth.
We lost track of the purpose and reason for life.
We began to forget our songs. We forgot our stories.
We could no longer see or hear our ancestors,
or talk with each other across the kitchen table.
Now Rabbit couldn't find a drink of fresh water.
The forests were being mowed down all over the world.
The earth was being destroyed to make more, and Rabbit had
   no place to play.
Rabbit's trick had backfired.

Rabbit tried to call the clay man back,
but when the clay man wouldn't listen,
Rabbit realized he'd made a clay man with no ears.

I was not brave.

I was pulled from my mother, whom I almost killed with the struggle. I was hooked up to a ventilator. I was dying even as I was being born. This continues to be a theme in my life, this struggle with transitions: between night and day, here and there, desert and water, earth and sky, and beginnings and endings. As I was being born, I had the same dying, gulping breaths as my father's last breaths when he died several years later, in a small Texas town near the water.

We are linked by water and fire.

My father and I surfaced in an ancient memory once when I was in my thirties. We lived by the water near a volcano. We who lived there had a long relationship with the spirit of the volcano. Our behavior broke the trust. We littered the land with trash and discord. We forgot to acknowledge the gifts. The volcano mountain blew with a terrible pressure. The earth rocked and fell open. Lava the color of fiery blood streamed toward us. Fire and ash rained down. We panicked for air.

The man who was now my father and I stumbled to the sea with our lungs on fire. I was his companion, friend, not the daughter I was to be in this life, this story. Many others rushed toward the sea to get away from the raining fire. We fell into a boat docked near shore, as did many others, more than the boat could carry. We attempted to move away from the falling ash, into the ocean, which was moving oddly in the disturbance. Hundreds were jumping into the water, clinging to the boat. I lost earth consciousness.

One version of the Mvskoke creation story begins with a volcano. It marked our journey from a place in the west. Sam Proctor, the *helis heya* or medicine maker of my tribal town, told me that in that time seven Hawaiian canoes came to shore. Those people became part of us. We walked east to more stable lands. A compassionate fire appeared before us to guide us. We made it to what is now known as the southeastern part of the United States.

Someone accompanies every soul from the other side when it enters this place. Usually it is an ancestor with whom that child shares traits and gifts.

My guardian remains, and reminds me of those older generations of Creek people who stayed close to the teachings, like my cousin John Jacobs of Holdenville, my beloved aunt Lois Harjo Ball, and George and Stella Coser, Sr. They speak softly, with kindness. They are quick with humor, and keep an open path. They have been tested with suffering and have responded with wisdom rather than bitterness. They teach by story, images, and songs. And they are respectful to mystery. They continue to remind me that it is best to walk this earthly path with *vnektckv*, compassion. All I have to do is remember them, and they stand in memory in a kind light.

▲   ▲   ▲

The next thing I remember, my mother is holding my small hands in hers, jitterbugging me across her spotless kitchen floor, the sun streaming in on beams of yellow starbursts.

What a beautiful being my mother was to me. I studied

her endlessly, every plane of her face, the light of her spirit, the flash, fall, and rise of her heart. In those earliest years, before I was five, I thrived in the home she and my father made. He worked as an airline mechanic. She was a magician to me. She took fabric with prints of toys and baby ducks and made new clothes for me and my brother, who was eighteen months younger. She took flour, sugar, eggs, spices, fat, and a hot oven and made cookies in shapes. She made music with her voice as she sang along with the radio, as she cooked and cleaned and took care of a household.

My father was more of a mystery. He lived most of the time in a farther-away realm more than he lived within the domestic universe of our home. When he was home from work, he moved through the house as if he were walking through water.

I adored my father and I feared him. When he'd lift me up to the sky with a laugh, I yearned to fly. I'd try, but I always disappointed him by crying out with fear of falling. He'd put me down and walk away. Later he'd pull me to his knee and circle me close to his heart. Despite the hurt that made him tight, I knew he loved me. And in the end, I was the one to help lead him through the door of earthly life to the other side.

My mother told me that one night not long after I was born she was waiting up for him in the living room. I was an infant, asleep in my bassinet. My father stumbled in the door. He was crazy drunk. He wrapped an arm around Mother's neck in a chokehold and told her that he would kill her if she didn't get in there and take care of the baby. She moved slowly and quietly, in shock, to pick me up. While he passed out in the bedroom she held and rocked me and sobbed quietly through the night. The next morning he had no recollection of his threat. As he begged my mother's forgiveness, he held us both in his arms. She stayed with him and would stay with him until I was eight years old because she loved him, though that night he broke her heart.

The heavy promise of snow wet the air, and my brother and I were jittery with anticipation. We wanted it to snow. We wanted our father to make it home with the Christmas tree.

The house smelled of gingerbread, and we'd eaten everything: the scraps of dough, raisin eyes, and fresh cookie shapes taken from the oven. We ran back and forth to the front window to watch for our father. Our baby sister stirred in her wrappings from her winter newborn nap. Every passing car and we were at the window again.

It was Saturday night, and our father had left late morning to pick up the Christmas tree. My brother kept asking our mother, "When's Daddy coming home?" And she always answered the same: "He'll be home any minute." She anxiously paced the kitchen, checking the baking sheets of cookies and chopping and frying the potatoes and meat. It was long past time for dinner, and we were hungry and cranky.

I set the table with plates and glasses while my brother seriously set the forks. At two years old, he was already our mother's "little man." He shadowed her, and usually she didn't mind, but tonight the baby was restless and there was no sign of our father. Since the baby had been born, my brother had been clingy and whiny. That night he was an outright nuisance. I had to keep shooing him from the coffee table covered with ornaments we'd unpacked for the Christmas tree. He'd already broken one of the glass soldiers, and I had cut my finger while sweeping up the slivers.

My brother asked yet again about our dad. I elbowed him a sharp one in the ribs. He cried, the baby cried, and I was in trouble for hitting again.

"As the older sister, you're to take care of your little brother. That's your responsibility." My mother shamed me. The sniffling boy nestled his head against her skirt as she soothed the sobbing infant and heated up the bottle of formula at the stove. She sent me to my room.

I refused to cry. I only cried when Daddy hit our mother. I felt terrible that I had hit my little brother. Shamed, as my mother said. It's a word I turned over and over in my mouth, and it didn't fit with the smell of gingerbread and frying potatoes. It didn't fit with the sparkle of the ornaments waiting to be put on the tree.

I went to my hiding place in the closet in the bedroom I shared with my brother. I pulled out my crayons.

I picked through them. Most were half eaten by my brother. He always managed to find them, no matter where I hid them. My latest hiding place was in the corner of the closet, in the back of the trunk my father used at school.

I drew on the wall. I imagined I was painting like my grandmother, whose painting of a warrior from our tribe hung in the living room. I looked at my drawings hidden behind our hanging clothes: here's the baby in her cradleboard, and here's my father hunting deer. I drew the outline of the Christmas tree. It had to be large, because it needed to hold all the ornaments and lights.

Before Daddy had left that morning, he had pulled down the box of Christmas lights and decorations from the hall closet. While the dough was cooling in the icebox so we could make shapes, our mother unwrapped the cotton batting protecting the delicate ornaments. There were shiny, mirrored balls, spirals of icicles, and ropes of tinsel to be wound around the tree. A few prized ornaments were of Wise Men, soldiers, and angels, and my brother and I had to be extra-careful with them. They broke easily.

"We decorate to welcome the baby Jesus," our mother instructed us. "He reminds us to love each other."

Last year at church I was Mary and stood as far away as I could from Joseph, a boy in Sunday school who picked his nose and cried for his mother. The baby Jesus had eyes that rolled back in his head. I refused to pick up the doll and cradle him in adoration. The other kids sang "Away in a Manger" as the parents smiled.

What was a manger, anyway?

The church people gave us white paper bags of oranges and ribbon Christmas candies. That was my favorite part.

My mother awakened me from the floor of the closet where I had fallen asleep. I was dreaming I was with my father in his boat at the lake. We couldn't move through the water because the lake was frozen. I was getting cold.

"It's snowing, baby," my mother whispered to me as she carried me to the window.

My little brother was asleep, curled up on his cot. He looked like one of the delicate angel ornaments. Baby was

sucking her hand as she dreamed and appeared to float in her
bassinet. There was still no tree, no father. I felt bad about
everything.

"I'm sorry, Mama."

"Shush," she cooed as she wiped the window free of frost.
"Look at all the snow."

We looked out together into the shining world. There was
magic in the whirling pictures the snow made. In the distance
I imagined my father dragging home a tree taller than the
house. He called out to my mother and me to open the door
as he hefted the trunk to his shoulder to bring it back home in
time for Christmas.

I was four years old when I woke up with muscle stiff-
ness, headache, and nausea—all the symptoms of polio. The
o's of the word *polio* rolled through my mouth like a game
of catch. The word sent hushed fear through the voices of
my parents as they moved about me, attempting to allevi-
ate my symptoms. My body was a hurting thing. Though I
tried, I could not leave my body by will.

I heard my mother on the phone with the doctor, her
fear tensing the mother-cord between us. I cried in pain, in
fear of the thoughts stabbing my parents' minds: *She could*
be crippled the rest of her life. She could die.

My father didn't know what to do. He knew how to
fix the car or his truck. He didn't know how to fix me, his
baby girl.

After hanging up with the doctor, my mother announced:
"We have to take her to the hospital, now."

My father left my side to get the car keys. A neighbor

who agreed to stay with my baby brother took instructions from my mother as she tightly rolled up my shivering body in a blanket.

I had the chills, and for a moment the chatter of my teeth distracted me. They made a rhythm. The rhythm pleased me. My father carried me to the car to take me to the hospital.

Polio was epidemic in the country. It caused paralysis and killed. My parents, the doctor, and the neighbor were frightened. I had entered a world in which everyone spoke softly, with trepidation, as if the sound of the word *polio* would call it into the house. In my parents' tribal traditions, the word, if spoken with intent, could call it here.

The hospital was a house of strangers. I was undressed and put in a gown, a diaper, and a crib. Not only was I sick, my status had dropped from girl to baby. My parents watched helplessly from a distance.

The transfer of power confused me. In this realm my parents were no longer the presiding gods.

A nurse in white carried me to a bare room for a spinal tap. I knew it was going to be bad when three people in uniforms came into the room to hold me down. I screamed as a needle went in. The spinal column carries personal essence back and forth between earth and sky. The spine is powerful and vulnerable. The procedure was excruciating.

I flailed as much with the fear as with the pain. Worse, I saw my mother's face across the room as it broke apart with my suffering. I didn't see my father there. He was standing out in the hallway, smoking a Lucky Strike cigarette. I can still hear the kind voice of a nurse attempting to reassure me by lying to me.

"It won't hurt too much. It will be over soon."

My parents gave me a white stuffed cat, then reluctantly left at the end of visiting hours.

I was bereft. The toy didn't replace my parents, but I needed that token of their love.

And I liked cats. My father was of the Tiger clan through his mother. This gave us a special connection with cats. Some of our family understand and speak cat language. Aunt Lois said her father had a black cat he fed special treats from the table. She said she told her father that he loved the cat more than her. Yet her father was of the Wind clan.

At four years old, when your parents are gone, they are gone forever. I mourned. I did not speak to the staff who came to check my vital signs or change me.

My parents arrived the next morning to take me home. The test results were negative. I did not have polio.

▲   ▲   ▲

It was shortly after the polio scare that I began to dream the alligator dream.

I am a young girl, between four and five years old. It's early in the morning. I delight in my feet touching the ground and in the plant beings who line the trail to the river. I breathe in playful energy from small, familiar winds as I walk to get water for the family. The winds appear to part the tall reeds through which I walk with my water jar.

An alligator whips me suddenly to the water and pulls me

*under. I struggle, and then I am gone. My passing from earth
is a quick choke. To my mourning family, my life has been
tragically ended. They did not see that I entered an underwa-
ter story to live with the alligators and become one of them.*

I had that dream many times throughout my childhood.
(My parents gave me a little brown dog, and I named him
Alligator. He lived for the thrill of chasing cars. No matter
where or how we penned him, when he heard a car, he was
gone. One day he finally caught a car and that was the end
of him.)

I believe now that I had the beginnings of polio. The alligators took it away. It is possible. This world is mysterious.

▲   ▲   ▲

In those early years I lived in a world of animal powers.
Most children do. In those years we are still close to the
door of knowing.

I got to know the trees, plants, and creatures around our
little white house with red trim built in the postwar boom.
Our house was one of many houses on the block. Each
centered on a square of lawn, each with a gas meter perched
near the street, in the place of a house altar.

I played with garter snakes, horned toads, frogs, June
bugs, and other creatures. Some of my favorite playmates
were roly-poly bugs. They busied about with several legs and
didn't trip themselves up. They protected themselves when
threatened by curling into a ball. As we played, I could see
the light shining around their little armored bodies.

I enjoyed lightning bugs, what others call fireflies, on

long summer nights. I saw them as tiny stars lighting up the intimate, close skies of childhood.

One morning I went with my mother across the street to visit her friend, another Cherokee woman. While my mother and her friend sat outside in chairs, catching up on neighborhood stories, I played in the thick clover that covered the lawn. I enjoyed listening to the rhythm of the women's stories, to the up-and-down flow of their talk and laughter.

As I played I caught bees in my hands. They became the people in my stories. I set them down on the ground as I imagined a house and the rooms of a house and the stories going on in the house. I moved them as I talked a story for them. One bee was the father, one the mother. The others were children, aunts, uncles, and grandchildren. In my mind I caught the rhythm of a story and rode it, unconsciously mimicking the story rhythm of my mother and her friend as they talked.

The bees were very cooperative. They always allowed me to hold them and move them about in my play. They would humor me, kindly, and then fly off. Then, that morning, I was startled from my play by the neighbor's alarmed voice.

"What are you doing? You'll be stung!"

I jumped. I took in her belief. Then I was stung. I stopped playing with the bees.

▲   ▲   ▲

My mother's mother, Leona May Baker, was Cherokee and Irish. This made for a potent meeting of storytellers, teachers, and musicians. She grew up in a traditional Cherokee family, in Cherokee lands near Moody, Oklahoma. My mother's father, Desmond Baker, was born of French and German immigrants. I do not know very much about them. He was a talker and threw out an unending string of talk as a lifeline to make it through the troubles and pressures of living. They were not book people. The only book they owned was the family Bible. In it was the family genealogy, written in careful ballpoint pen. Every name and date was a gateway to a story.

My grandmother used to dream stories as long as novels, said my mother. She used them to get the children into bed at night. They were thrilling and dramatic. She was skillful at timing, ending each episode at a critical juncture so the children were kept in suspense until the next night. My mother says she would think of the story all day long, eager for bedtime. It was a major undertaking to get seven children—six boys and one girl—tucked in at night. If they cooperated, they were rewarded with the next segment in the serial.

I can see them lined up together on the floor, wrapped in their pallets of handed-down blankets and quilts in the abandoned two-story house they lived in one winter when the family was destitute. No one else would go near the house, much less live in it, because the house was haunted. The family had no place else to go, and my mother's father was away working on the railroad.

My mother remembers wandering far to gather firewood. It was record-breaking cold that winter and most of the wood nearby had been picked off. To keep warm, the family blocked off most of the rest of the house and stayed in the room with the fireplace.

Every night the ghosts of the house would assemble for the party upstairs. My mother said she'd hear the tinkling keys of an old-time piano. Then she would hear the shuffle and slap of the deal of the cards, and the sighs and exclamations of the card players. The same party went on every night. The voices would start at a low, conversational rumble and then build as the night went on and they had more to drink, until a fight would break out. Then someone would fire a gunshot, and then the family would hear the strange bump of a dead body being dragged down the stairs. My mother said it terrified her, no matter how many times it happened.

In one story that hides out in the corner of family memory, a man comes home from working on the railroad all winter. It was a rough winter made by swinging a hammer through wind, ice, and rain. He carefully saves money for his family, though he does succumb to a few trips into town to gamble and drink with his friends, to see a woman. He's not a drinker or gambler by nature. He can take it or leave it. He has seven children at home. When he returns with enough cash to rent a place, buy new shoes for everyone and food, he discovers his wife is pregnant with a baby that is not his child. He beats her in a rage. She miscarries the child. Then he drags her into the path of an oncoming train and holds her there. The children watch in horror as their parents struggle on the tracks. As the train bears down on them, their father pushes their mother off the tracks and leaps away at the last possible second. They all go home. They continue to live as if the story never happened.

I remember following my mother about the house as she got ready to go out with my father for the night. I'd admire the red satin, the black velvet fabric, and the patterns of sequins of her party clothes as she bathed and dressed. I'd perch on the edge of the bathtub as she relaxed and soaked in a bubble bath, careful not to elbow her ashtray into the water. I'd try on her heels and pretend to be her. I knew she was beautiful to others. I kept track of every small increment of information as I watched my parents to gauge the emotional atmosphere of the house, to calculate what might happen.

Then I'd follow her as she dried, applied lotion, and dressed. I helped as she slipped on each layer, including the requisite girdle. She'd clip on her hosiery. I'd pick through her box of jewelry while she patted on her Max Factor makeup and drew on her red lipstick picked from the lineup of lipsticks on her dresser. When she put on her heels, my short, feisty mother became tall and elegant. She would then spray on White Shoulders perfume.

"How do I look, baby?"

I adored my mother. She was beautiful in jeans and a crisp-ironed blouse. She was beautiful dressed like the movie stars she and her friends admired.

As I would walk out of my mother's bedroom, I might hear Patsy Cline singing "I Fall to Pieces." My mother would sing along with Patsy as my father would take his keys out of his jacket and hold open the door for her. He'd carry a fifth from the bootlegger next door. He'd take a swig while my mother gave instructions to the babysitter. I remember whimpering because I knew that the magic of beauty is dangerous. It is easily taken apart and destroyed. I had seen it happen other times when my parents came home, bringing the party with them. I had seen her dresses ripped. I had seen the jewelry and lipsticks scattered and broken by my father's rage.

▲　▲　▲

Once my mother recorded one of her original songs, "Weeping Willow," on vinyl. I remember the day she shared it with her friends in the neighborhood. I can see her holding the circle of pressed dreams in her hands. I hear the crackle of her singing on the phonograph after she has set the needle down on the spinning disk. Ice clinks in glasses as her friends fill their drinks, the smoke from their cigarettes twining around their heads while they gather at the kitchen table to celebrate and to share what they've gleaned while story-gathering, so many stories of the loss and gain of power through family. My mother's story of the pressing of one of her songs was unusual, something to take note of in the field of the domestically ordinary. I was proud for her.

I wanted to make music like my mother. I liked that you could hold music in your hands. It was like holding a spinning world.

▲　▲　▲

My mother was born with a caul over her face, which meant that she had second sight. She did have an uncanny sense of knowing, especially when it came to the fortune of others. She said she could always pick a hit song when she heard the melody.

When I was about ten years old, I was given a Ouija board as a gift. When my mother and I touched the planchette, a triangular board with an opening to see letters or numbers beneath, it flew. It spelled out names, dates, and answers. And the answers were right. We became a team, reading for neighbor women who would come by and ask questions.

"When will my husband get out of jail?"

"Will I get the job I want?"

"When will I get married?"

We stopped when the energy around the board became strange, even frightening. Whatever was giving us answers became demanding and wanted more time and attention. I threw the board out.

▲　▲　▲

Like my father, I was not fully pressed into the place and time into which I was born. I remember my spirit rising up to follow a path of moonlight, looking over my shoulder to see my pajama-clad body in my crib, and, as I grew older, in my army cot. Even before birth, as my spirit prepared to enter my developing body, it wandered great distances from my mother and father.

In those earliest years, before language, I brought back images of sarcophagi in Egypt. I carried long story sequences of those times, which I do not remember now. One of the oldest stories took place in lower Nubia and involved a very cruel imprisonment. People were literally buried alive, standing up. I can still see the rows of eyes looking out. They haunted me for many nights. I can still see them in a stark, unrelenting sunlight, suffering without water. They were there because they did not agree with the prevailing government.

And I visited the moon. My teacher or guardian sometimes accompanied me, or met me there.

This kind of story travel was normal for me. I often felt more awake in my dreaming life than I did in this corporeal reality. I still do. My travel through story realms stopped when I started public school. It was also at this time that I began attending an evangelical church. Church members caught us as we left the doors of the public school, giving out candy suckers attached to fliers advertising vacation Bible school. I wanted more candy. I was always up for stories.

In church I was taught that anything visionary on a personal level, especially in girls or women, was evil and most likely of the devil. I became fearful of those abilities. I closed the door.

▲   ▲   ▲

In the last long summer dusk before I started elementary school, I was playing in the yard with my brother and the neighbor children. There was no end to that day; it is still dusk in memory.

I was five years old. I was swinging in the trees, jumping over the gas meter. There were somersaults, tag, bees, clover, the red porch, and the possibility of watermelon and homemade ice cream. There was scramble of ball, running and tackling. There were horned toads, toads to give you warts, June bugs and lightning bugs. There were snakes to find in the grass. I liked their writhing aliveness, their black no-question eyes, and their tongues that flashed like lightning. They smelled like cool melon, stronger toward dusk and dew.

And then my mother interrupted the party with a command: "Joy! Come in here right now and put on a shirt."

I bristled with injustice.

"Why doesn't my brother have to come in and put on a shirt?"

"He's a boy."

"But we look the same."

"Don't argue with me, girl, or I'll have you pick a switch."

I went inside to put on a shirt. I knew better than to talk back. In that small moment the earthy delight of being five years old, of being utterly body and breath, came falling down.

I saw the Christian law of forthright tied-tight shoes ahead of me. I saw scratchy lace and flounce, my mother's girding girdles, the shame of "down there," the bowed heads, and the closed doors of house or church.

As I pulled my T-shirt over my head to cover my girl-shame, I decided that though temporarily I had to acquiesce, I would have nothing to do with it. I would find a way, my way.

I ran back outside into the flare of twilight to join my brother and our friends, and jumped back into our game of war.

▲   ▲   ▲

By the time I started school the family included two more children, another sister and a brother.

In kindergarten the students were divided into groups after naptime and sent to various activity stations around the spacious classroom. The activities varied from drawing to jumping rope to stringing beads. The two kind, elderly teachers who wore matronly dresses and black boxy shoes with laces liked to see the "cute little Indian girl" stringing beads, so I was often first assigned to play there.

Drawing was my favorite station. I loved the smell of crayons on newsprint. I smelled each crayon before using it and felt each color as a friendly field of possibility. One day I lost myself in a drawing as I discovered a design similar to the joined-hands circle of paper dolls made by cutting a folded sheet of paper. When I glanced up and around the table, I noticed that the other children were all drawing the same house, the same lollipop tree, and the same sun with a smiling face. I broke through my shyness and asked, "Why are you copying each other?"

The other children looked at me, then at my drawing. They began copying me.

For me drawing was dreaming on paper. I didn't always know what was going to appear there. I followed the instinct of color, of line. I understood there were many kinds of houses. Some did not exist in the city in which I lived. The one I used to draw again and again was a round house with a tree at the center. The stairs wound around the outside of the house. When I was about four years old I had become obsessed with drawing igloo houses. I drew them in chalk all over the slate walls of our garage. Along with them I drew babies wrapped tight in fur coverings.

After I asked that question of the other children in the kindergarten classroom I had a sense of knowing that my path would most likely veer from everyone else's. I understood in a flash, without words, that if I did not follow my path, I would suffer, even as I would suffer for following it. The latter suffering was preferable.

I kept drawing, and kept the rest of my questions to myself.

▲ ▲ ▲

The next year, in first grade, my decision to color a ghost green instead of leaving it the off-white of newsprint set off a controversy in our small classroom. Students gathered around my desk to confront me.

"A ghost can only be white," they demanded.

I was going to get in trouble and they were hanging close to see what would happen.

"Have you ever seen a ghost?" I asked. I did not want to tell them that I had seen how a green ball of energy could give people pneumonia. This was a classroom of Weekly Readers, of letters and numbers in order from A to Z, one to twenty. It was Dick and Jane, Spot, Puff, and Sally from our readers. What I had seen did not fit into this kind of place.

When the children ran to the teacher to report my coloring mistake, she told the children to sit down and get back to work. I thank her for that, now.

I did not redo my coloring. I made note of how much

it bothered my classmates that someone had gone "outside the lines."

I saw the eyes of the prisoners who had gone against the story of their captors.

I also noted that though I was in a classroom of both native and white students, I was the only child who colored in the skin of my figures. I colored them orange, the closest color I could find in my box of eight crayons to capture the skin tones of my mother and father.

It was in that same classroom I learned to read. The moment the letters became sounds and sounds became stories and poems I lit up, especially when I saw the rows and rows of books in the classroom and the library. Each book was its own matrix and contained a world you could carry in your hands. I read all of the books in the first-grade classroom, then started on the books in the second-grade classroom.

When I was eight years old my mother gave me a copy of Louis Untermeyer's *Golden Books Family Treasury of Poetry* for my birthday. I loved poetry. It was singing on paper. And to open that book was to disappear into many dream worlds, like the ones I had left behind after I started school and began to perfect language.

The collection was generous in scope and included everyone from Elizabeth Bishop and her spectacular poem "The Fish" to William Blake's "The Tiger" and the hypnotic lines "Tiger, tiger, burning bright/In the forests of the night"; to Emily Dickinson ("I'm nobody! Who are you?") and Lewis Carroll's "The Crocodile" ("How doth the little crocodile/Improve his shining tail").

Those poems, taken as a group, summed up my soul at that crucial moment in my personal history. My father was out with girlfriends or coming home drunk and fighting my mother. He was the "tiger, tiger, burning bright."

My parents were in the process of a difficult divorce. My escape was remembering fishing with my grandfather the summer before and the "rainbow, rainbow, rainbow" of the caught fish glittering in the afternoon sunlight.

I saw the police come to the house. My father staggered in and out with his belongings, with the smell of other women like strange clouds on his clothes.

My mother confided my father's shortcomings in me and I advised her to leave my father. I felt like I was "nobody— who are you?"

My father disappeared. And so did I in this world without father. Emptiness took the place of everything I had known to be true.

With the alligators or the crocodile, I could find refuge in another realm below this one. There are underground cities, other peoples.

Even though I was the oldest female in my family, I didn't gather and mother my brothers and sister when my father left. I dove into the other realm, and everyone was left to fend for him- or herself.

▲　▲　▲

In one of my last childhood memories of my father, I was a brown child wearing one of those dollar-apiece sun suits made of cheap polished cotton that fades after the first wash. It was tied at my shoulders. Two blue-black braids hung down my back. I was sweaty from running; my knees were scraped from jumping and falling.

I leaned against my father. I adored him. And I was afraid of him. Together both of those places lived within me.

I looked up toward his face and read his lips for mood. I read for love or imminent cruelty. He was laughing and making a joke with his friends. Yeasty beer smell mixed with father sweat. He pulled me to his lap. I heard his heart beating. I tapped the rhythm on his pressed-jean thigh. I was always tapping rhythms. I counted.

One, and ah. Two, and ah. Three, and ah.

Our heartbeats are numbered. We have only so many allotted. When we use them up, we die. How many did my father have? How many did I have?

▲   ▲   ▲

The kitchen chairs were red vinyl. The ice cream churn was propped by the back steps with a pile of blankets, waiting for my father to make ice cream for us as he promised. The story veers from here.

In one version my father laughed as he stood up to make the ice cream. We children followed him, jumping up and down in excitement and anticipation. I was the oldest, the one who got to sit on the blankets that covered the churn. He turned and turned the crank until the ice cream was made. My mother dipped us each a bowl of delicately flavored ice cream made from fresh peaches. We sat out on the steps and ate of the sweetness until we could eat no more.

In the other version, my father continued his drinking party. The house was a roar of music and bravado. We were no longer in the yellow kitchen with my mother's plants that wound around the windows, hundreds of leaves and vines, in response to her singing.

We were in the alternate realm of the kitchen. It was the kitchen of hunting rifles, deer blood, and car parts soaking in grease. It was a house turned over in the dark.

My father would get angry. He would get angry because his mother died of tuberculosis when he was a baby, because his father beat him, because he was treated like an Indian man in lands that were stolen away along with everything else.

He would punch and kick in anger because something in the house was not right: *The dinner is not right, my wife is not right, and where are the children? What's wrong with them? Aren't they in bed yet?*

It will never be right as long as you are angry, I wanted to say, but who was I to say, because I was a child. And because I was a child I cowered under the table to hide when he started coming my way in anger. My cowering made him even angrier, because I was not brave at all.

NORTH

North is the direction where the difficult teachers live. This is the direction of cold winds. The color is white, sharp and bare. It is the direction marked by the full moon showing the way through the snow. It is prophecy.

And whom do I call my enemy?
An enemy must be worthy of engagement.
I turn in the direction of the sun and keep walking.
It's the heart that asks the question, not my furious mind.
The heart is the smaller cousin of the sun.
It sees and knows everything.
It hears the gnashing even as it hears the blessing.
The door to the mind should open only from the heart.
An enemy who gets in risks the danger of becoming a friend.

After we lost my father when my parents divorced, my mother and our family of four children kept going, though we floated in the chaos of unknowing. Our mother worked several jobs. When word got out that our beautiful mother was single, men began showing up to court her. Most she dismissed. We children liked the Indian bull rider missing two fingers best. He showed us how to loop a rope, throw a lasso. We loved the twangy beat of his country guitar, his kind shine.

There was an angular preacher who wore black. He smelled sour and lonely. He carried a switch for beating behind his back. My mother did not invite him to return. In fact, she hadn't invited him at all.

The last man who courted our mother was seventeen years older. He charmed her and us. He gave me a pair of skates. He took us for rides that ended in hamburgers and shakes. He sang songs and smiled with his eyes. He'd been watching our mother for some time.

He married our mother in a ceremony without us.

We moved from our childhood home with its familiar trees, plants, and creatures. We left our friends, our school, and the memories that were rooted there. As we drove away from the house we had known as our own, I disappeared into a cloud of sullen mourning.

We moved to a house with four bedrooms that my mother and stepfather found together on "Independence" Street. What irony. In that house I had nightmares and premonitions of evil. The first night there, with unpacked boxes surrounding me in the room I was to share with my sister, I woke up in the midst of a struggle with a dark being. I cried out for my mother. No one came. I remember being reprimanded by my stepfather the next morning. I was never to disturb their sleep in the night again. Any pretense of nice ended there.

The next Saturday morning I followed my five-year-old sister's cries to the kitchen and found her being held aloft by one leg by my stepfather. I froze in terror. My brother closest in age stood with me.

"This is what will happen to you if you misbehave." He swung our sister around.

He unbuckled and pulled off his belt in one slick motion. I still see the sweat crescents under the arms of his work shirt. I hear him grunt with the effort as he whips her.

When he was done he put her down, then slid the belt back carefully around his girth. His buckle made a satisfied click. Then he went into the living room, back to watching golf on the television.

I ran to tell my mother about the belt-buckle marks on the baby's leg.

I imagine our mother hadn't come out at the sound of the ruckus because she assumed she was finally getting help with disciplining us. The divorce and then the move had stirred up her gang of children. We were confused and acting out. She naturally believed that if he was spanking one of us, it was because we needed it. He'd signed on to be her partner in marriage.

My mother scooped up her bruised baby, who was hiccuping with tears. When she saw the marks, she was furious. She walked into the living room to confront her husband. I followed close behind her, trying to stay in her shadow so he couldn't see me.

He denied hitting my sister with the belt buckle, though the mark was clearly delineated on her leg. He called me a liar. Then he and my mother went back to their room for the rest of the afternoon. It was the last time he hit my sister, but after that he had it in for me.

I begged my mother to leave him. I was still upset about the succession of events that had led us to this house of bad spirits and pain. There were literally hundreds of snakes in the yard. We were in the middle of one of those fairy tales that was rolling toward a nasty end. The pressure kept me up at night. From the time our stepfather married and moved us until the day I left home as a teenager, I kept sentry at night. I would doze lightly or not at all until I heard and saw the sun coming up over the horizon. Then I would sleep.

My mother confided that there was no way we could leave. He said he would kill her and her children if she divorced him. He'd leave our bodies in a burning house. He said it would look like an accident. No one would ever know. We both knew he would do it.

▲   ▲   ▲

One night I woke up to a scuffle in the living room. My mother had just come in from her weekly date of playing shuffleboard at the bar with her girlfriends. I heard my stepfather grilling her. I heard my mother protesting and weeping. My sister slept peacefully beside me. My brothers were in their room. I wondered if they heard anything.

"Who were you with?" my stepfather demanded.

"I was partying with my girlfriends. You know I don't have anyone else."

"If you want to party, we'll have a party right here."

I wound tighter, ready to leap to save her. I heard him methodically popping open beers with a church key, one after another, and pouring beer down her throat and over her clothes. I heard ripping. My mother kept saying it wouldn't happen again. *It won't happen again. It won't happen again.*

Then it was quiet. It was quiet until dawn, and then I got up for school.

After that, my mother's few girlfriends called or came by only when my stepfather wasn't around. She never went out except for work or to do errands he had specifically approved. He watched and marked her every step, her every word.

In those times there were no domestic abuse shelters. If either my mother or I had been brave enough to report him, the authorities would have accepted his word over ours because he was an employed white man. We would have been forced back with no protection, and he would have been given tacit permission to keep us in line.

▲   ▲   ▲

I never heard my mother sing much anymore. Her singing used to fill the house. We would turn up the radio and dance to rock-and-roll together. Our house now was quiet with our labor to keep it in order. My sister and I had the bulk of the duties, because we were female. I was in charge of cleaning, doing laundry, including the ironing for the family, washing dishes, and child care. Our brothers emptied the trash and mowed the lawn. I tried making a case for rotating duties. I didn't feel it was a fair distribution. There was no negotiating.

Our mother worked hard and long hours in restaurants, either cooking or waitressing or both. Our stepfather contributed only his share of the mortgage. Our mother paid for everything else. She bought all groceries, food, and clothes. Our father could not be found for child support.

The last and only time I saw my mother sing publicly was shortly after she and my stepfather got together.

Leon McAuliffe and His Cimarron Boys were gigging at a huge community picnic near the border of Arkansas and Oklahoma, not far from where my mother grew up. McAuliffe was known for his steel guitar solos, especially for playing with Bob Wills and His Texas Playboys. That McAuliffe had agreed to let my mother sit in for one of her original songs was a big deal. This had been her life. The bandleader Ernie Fields had even arranged one of her songs for his orchestra.

There was tension in the car as my stepfather drove us the two hours to the event. My mother sat up front with him, the four of us children crowded in the back. She was nervous. She hadn't sung with a band for a few years. She was dressed for her musical coming-out party in satin, frills, and perfume.

My stepfather was already jealous and ready to go at someone because his wife, who was younger than he was, looked so pretty. She didn't look like a jailed, beleaguered mother of four children. I was wary, because I knew our stepfather would make her pay.

My grandfather—my mother's father—met us there. I sat next to him as I balanced my box of greasy fried chicken on my lap. I was nervous for my mother. I embodied her every emotional knot and fear. I wanted this opportunity to be good for her. I wanted to protect her.

I remember the moment she was called up to the stand to sing. My heart leaped as she stood up. She looked beautiful as she took the stage with Leon and the boys. At first she appeared startled, as if she had just escaped from a dark box. As the intro bars of the music started, my mother appeared tentative, nervous, but then she caught hold. I heard the mother who held my hands and sang and danced in the kitchen with her plants all around. I felt her spirit reach up and touch the sun when she sang.

And then, too quickly, it was over. Everyone clapped. My mother smiled a big smile as she came down from the stage.

I didn't want to go back with my stepfather and mother. I wanted to stay with my grandfather. I clung to him.

I believed I was the favorite of all his grandchildren. Maybe all of us believed we were the favorite. He peeled apples for us. He made us a tree swing.

I was his dump companion. I loved to search the landfill at the edge of his small town with him. We'd find all sorts of treasure there: chairs with seats that could be woven back into place, toys with an eye or a fender missing, all usable stuff.

Other days we'd go to the spring to fetch water. I can

still taste the fresh, clean water emerging from stones. Or we'd go fishing. He'd hook my bait and patiently unhook my line from the trees, his overalls, and anywhere else it landed from my faulty casting. Once in a while he'd even pull a fish off.

I didn't want to go home because I knew my mother would have hell to pay. We would all pay, because we children were her accomplices. I remember looking back at my grandfather as my stepfather rushed our mother and us out of there.

My stepfather belittled my mother as we drove back home.

The car filled with ugliness.

When we got home there was no celebration, as there should have been. My mother disappeared into their room and slept and slept for what seemed like years.

▲   ▲   ▲

I imagine this place in the story as a long silence. It is an eternity of gray skies. It runs the length of late elementary school through adolescence. I do recall bright moments: getting the understudy for a part in an operetta based on the story of Cinderella, climbing and running through the quarry behind the elementary school with my friends, and having boxing bouts with the neighborhood boys. I was good at it.

There were three strange events during this time that baffled me.

I always had pets. My mother said I had a way with animals. One was a kissing fish I kept in a goldfish bowl. I hadn't had the fish long before I began to realize it was too large for the depth of the bowl. It kept flipping itself out. One afternoon I accidentally stepped on the fish as I tried to capture it and return it to water. It flattened and bled. I carefully picked it up and returned it to the water. The fish floated on its side, nearly dead. I began to pray. I went deep into prayer for the life of this fish. I felt my heart open and the heart of the fish open. I felt at peace.

I took a break to sweep. When I returned, the fish had righted itself and was swimming in healthy circles around the bowl. In that small moment, I felt the presence of the sacred, a force as real and apparent as anything else in the world, present and alive, as if it were breathing. I wanted to catch hold, to remember utterly and never forget. But the current of hard reality reasserted itself. I had to have the house cleaned just right or my stepfather would punish me. So I continued on my path of forgetfulness.

One night my mother was still working and my stepfather was out bowling or at an Elks club meeting. We had a babysitter who was watching television in the living room. A light brighter than any light I'd ever seen appeared at the head of my bed. It grew larger and larger, and as it grew it terrified me. It was not evil, like the darkness that plagued the house and our family. The light was beautiful. Even so, I called out fearfully. The babysitter came running and turned on the yellowish bedroom light. The white light disappeared. I tried to explain what I had seen, but there were no words, just as words stumble inadequately now. She told me to get to sleep and clicked off the room light. I lay there and wondered at what I had seen. I wanted it to come back, yet I was fearful of its returning and lay there with the covers pulled up to eye level.

When I was ten, my mother and I stayed up to monitor Hurricane Carla. It took a rare path, tearing up the entire coastline of Texas before heading north to Tulsa. My step-father was out for the evening. I inwardly rejoiced that my mother and I had a rare evening alone. The atmosphere of the storm was a huge aura of whirling particles. It stirred up danger in us.

We walked through the house, checking doors and windows. The younger children were all in bed, sleeping. We sat together and listened as the winds began slamming the city. We knew about tornadoes. They were quirky and strange creatures. I had watched one descend from a bruised sky, approach our neighborhood. It skipped us and tore up trees and cars on the next block, tossed them into the sky as if they were toys.

We were uncertain what this hurricane would do. It had lost force as it traveled north. We listened to reports on the radio as to the storm's progress and sang along with the radio to songs we knew. Suddenly a ball of fire sizzled and crackled as it flew from the roof of the kitchen through the house. It disappeared down the hall, and then it was gone. I felt a panicked doom. The sign was ominous.

Then my stepfather drove up, and my mother didn't have to remind me to hurry to my room. We would both have been in trouble if I had been up past bedtime. And he did not like us spending time together. I escaped to my room just as the front door opened.

The water monster lived at the bottom of the lake. He didn't disappear in the age of reason. He remained a mystery that never happened.

In the muggy lake was the girl I was at sixteen. The story at the surface said she got there by car accident, or by drowning while drinking. Whatever it was, they'd say, it was an accident.

The story was not an accident, nor was the existence of the water monster. It lived in the memory of the people as they carried the burden of the myth from Alabama to Oklahoma. Each reluctant step on the trail impressed memory into the broken heart, and no one ever forgot it.

When I walked the stairway of water into the abyss, I returned as the wife of the water monster, wearing a blanket of time decorated with swatches of cloth and feathers from our favorite birds.

The stories of the battle of the water monster were forever ongoing. Those stories seeped into my blood since infancy like deer gravy, so when the water monster appeared as the most handsome man in the tribe, or of any band whose visits I'd been witness to since childhood, how could I resist?

The first time he appeared I carried my baby sister on my back as I went to get water. She laughed at a woodpecker flitting like a small red sun above us, and before I could deter the symbol we were in it.

My body was already on fire with the explosion of womanhood as if I were flint, hot stone, and when he stepped out of the water he was the first myth I had ever seen uncovered. I surprised him in a human moment.

My baby sister's cry pinched reality. The red bird was a warning of disjuncture in the brimming sky.

What I had seen there in the body beyond the water needed the words of holy recounting.

I ran back to the village drenched in salt and sky. How could I explain the water jar left empty by the river to my mother, who deciphered my burning lips as shame?

My imagination swallowed me like a mica chip. In it, I had seen the water monster fighting with lightning. He broke trees, stirred up killer winds. In it, I had lost my brother to a spear of flame. I saw my beloved there, hidden in the skin of the suddenly vulnerable.

I was taken with a fever and nothing cured it until I dreamed my fiery body dipped in the river where it fed into the lake.

My father carried me as if I were newborn, as if he were presenting me once more to the world. And when he dipped me I was pronounced healed.

My parents immediately made plans to marry me to an important man who was years older and would provide me with everything I needed to survive in this world.

It was a world I could no longer perceive. I had been blinded, when I was most in need of a drink, by a man who was not a man. He stole my secrets, those created at the brink of language.

When I disappeared it was in a storm that destroyed the houses of my relatives. My baby sister was found sucking on her hand in the crook of an oak.

And though it may have appeared otherwise, I did not go willingly. That night when I had seen my story strung on the shell belt of my ancestors, I was standing next to a man who could not look me in the eye.

The oldest woman in the tribe wanted to remember me

as the girl who disobeyed, who gave in to her desires before
marriage and was destroyed by the monster disguised as the
seductive warrior.

    Others saw the car I was driving as it drove into the lake
early one morning, the time the carriers of tradition wake up,
before the sun or the appearance of red birds. They found the
empty six-pack on the sandy shores of the lake.

    The power of the victim is a power that will always be
reckoned with, one way or the other. When the proverbial
sixteen-year-old woman walked down to the lake, within her
were all the sixteen-year-old women who had questioned their
power from time before time.

    Years later, she walked out of the lake and headed for
town. No one recognized her. The story of the girl and the
water monster was a story no one told anymore.

My stepfather was paying more and more attention to
me as I grew into womanhood. I did everything I could to
stay out of his way. I did not want his eyes on me.

    Like most teenage girls, I felt sensual and awkward all at
once. My body had its own mind, its own wisdom. I was
tethered to its cycles. I was up and I was down.

    I was attractive: I watched a boy wreck his car because
he was staring at me. I was ugly: I had had a front tooth
missing from the time I was seven. I cracked it while leap-
ing on furniture to catch my brother while we were in
the care of a babysitter. It was too expensive to replace the
tooth properly. Without a front tooth, I learned to keep my
mouth shut and my head down.

    My head was often in my sketchbook. I sketched fashions. I made my own clothes. My designs and ideas would show up months later on the pages of fashion magazines, said my mother.

I made good grades. School was a refuge from home. I found friends who did not know my house or my family because they did not live nearby. I made friends across the various islands of school cultures, from the elite socs, who had everything from looks to money, to the renegade greasers, who could usually be found slinking up against the back fence, smoking. My friends were other Indian students as well as non-Indian students. I defied categories. I was considered "the brain" and "the artist" all at once.

My stepfather watched me closely. I felt like prey. I had to be stealthy. I was careful not to be anywhere near him alone. I didn't want to be anywhere that he might be tempted to touch me in any manner.

I slipped up, because he found my hidden diary, broke the lock, and read aloud from it in front of the family. He read my day-to-day musings. They were small things, but they were mine and they were meant to be private.

I walked home with my friends and saved my bus money. Bought gloss.
Pepsi and a peanut butter cup for lunch.
Saturday at the library.
I imagined a kiss. Forever.
DK and Me. 2 Young 2 Be Together.
Bee To Gather.
"I shall love thee better after death."
Elizabeth Barrett Browning so cool.

He read those words with great delight. I was humili-
ated. Violated. I swore to myself I would never write anything again.

I had no thoughts of becoming a writer, though I
checked out my quota of books every week from the local
branch of the library, located in the strip mall down the
road. I checked out books on physics, fat novels I could
loll around in—from Louisa May Alcott, Dickens to cheap
popular stuff—paranormal and ghost reportage, and human
anatomy books. I was the library reference person for my
friends. They asked questions about sex, unicorns, and religion, and I would look them up.

I belonged to the Columbia House Record Club. I
bought recordings with money I made from my jobs.
I baby-sat, I took in ironing, and one summer I took a
job busing and washing dishes at the restaurant where my
mother cooked.

In those junior high years I went for bands like the Yard-
birds and the Byrds. I discovered Bizet's *Carmen*. I even
liked the gummy pop of the Monkees' music. They were
easy to sing. And always Motown.

If my mother was fire and my father was water, I was a
little of each. My spirit found refuge in those watery realms.
I too was looking for a vision that would lead me free of the
domestic prison our home had become with my stepfather.
Or rather, vision was looking for me, and I was still hiding
and afraid. It carried responsibility.

I was fire and I was confused about the fire in my body.
I was told it was wrong by the church to feel desire, yet
I pondered on how desire must have been created by the

same god that I was told created everything in the world. Power and shame tumbled together.

I created constantly. I drew, took photographs, and I loved to sing.

▲ ▲ ▲

In the house, everything stopped when we heard my stepfather's car pull up into the drive after he got off work around four o'clock. Everyone hid outside or in their rooms. When I heard his car I'd turn off the record player, stop singing or dancing, and find a broom or a rag and clean, even though I had usually finished cleaning by then.

One afternoon I forgot the time. I was singing along with an album spinning on my record player when the door of my bedroom burst open. My stepfather stood with his belt in his hand. He slackened and popped it forcefully. He forbade me ever to sing in the house again. Then he beat me.

I stopped singing. I didn't write. I kept sketchbooks, made designs, and my art was even picked for student exhibitions, but for all that imagination, I couldn't imagine another way through, or a way out.

▲ ▲ ▲

I was excited to start all over in a new school at the beginning of my first year at Will Rogers High. And like every first day of school since kindergarten, I determined to do my best as I opened up my new pads of paper, sharpened my new pencils, lined up my new pens and packed them in my school bag.

Several junior high classes fed into the school. It was

massive. At every bell students jammed the halls, streaming to make it to the next class. Now and then I waved to someone I knew and added my greeting to the din of voices. I'd always liked the discipline and ritual of learning. To know something gave me more ability to move within my mind. There was more territory to contemplate. There were more doors. Where I got stuck was in wanting to perfect what I learned; instead, we had to keep going, imperfect, from one assignment or set of lessons to the next. There was always something more to know.

And what happened, I wondered, if you read and took in every book in every library of the world, learned the name of every seashell, every war, and could quote every line of poetry? What would you do with all that knowing? Would it be the kind of knowledge that could free you? Or would infinite knowledge bind you with the junky posturing of human beings who didn't appear to be that wise? And who decided what knowledge was important to know and understand?

I saw a posted flier about upcoming auditions for the next school play. I decided to challenge myself. I was terrified about standing in front of juniors and seniors and auditioning. Yet I was compelled. The stage was a place where magic could happen that could take you far away. Countries could rise up and be destroyed. Lovers could defy obstacles. Some would die, while others would find a way through the abyss.

My mother gave me permission to stay after school for the meeting to get script pages and be assigned a tryout time. Because I would miss the bus, I would have to walk the two miles home. I didn't mind. The walk home would give me rare time to myself. I hoarded time alone and liked best spending it outside, in music, or buried in a book.

I liked being with my thoughts—which ran between sensual fantasy and conjecture over the nature of reality. What is eternity? And what about the presence of Time? Is Time a being who can be appeased? Or is Time a tyrant? And will I ever find love? Love was something distant. I did not associate it with the fumbles of boys who were only looking for quick gratification. I wanted someone to come and find me and take me away.

Though I rarely spoke up in my classes, I had a voice that carried. When I was in plays in elementary school, I loved the ritual preparations of rehearsal and finally the test of performance. I was able to escape from the hard reality of the Oklahoma of stolen Indian lands and the self-righteous religious right.

The last play I had been in was in sixth grade. In junior high there had been no theater, except the shot-through hormone dramas that played out through all the linked social circles.

I walked home after the high school theater meeting excited and nervous. I patted my bag, making sure my script pages with my tryout time scribbled on it were there. I admired the trees that lined the streets in the upper-class neighborhoods near the high school. I breathed in air that felt like freedom. I imagined that one day I might even live in a neighborhood like this. My father had grown up in a house of twenty-one rooms in Okmulgee, a house bought by Indian oil money.

As I drew closer to our block, the houses were smaller, poorer. Though my stepfather was a house painter, our house was peeling and appeared ragged and in need of repair. The yard was barren and wild. Our house was noticeably the shabbiest house on the block.

I could have taken initiative with the yard, but I always lost energy when I stepped into the aura of the house. I struggled with lethargy and often had to force myself through chores and obligations.

I felt a warning in my gut. My stepfather's car was in the drive. I tried to disarm the knowing.

The knowing was a powerful warning system that stepped forth when I was in danger. Still, I often disregarded it. I'd been asked by a boy a few years older than me to go for a walk behind the grounds of the teen recreation center. My knowing said to me in a loud, distinct voice, *Do not walk alone with this boy. To do so would put you in danger.* I must be imagining things, I said to myself. I walked with him. He knocked me down and attempted to rape me. Someone came on us and I leaped up and got away.

The knowing was always right. It could never be disarmed. It stood watch over me.

Still, I tried. I told the knowing to remember that my stepfather could be nice sometimes. He sang show tunes to my mother. The knowing didn't respond. Truth does not lower itself to small-time arguments or skirmishes.

But, I argued with myself, you never knew what would happen. He could uncover or invent a transgression of weeks or months before and off would come his belt if he needed an excuse to hit you. Or, once when I thought I would get in trouble for climbing into the space between the ceiling and the roof and falling through into the living room, he just laughed.

I hugged my bag under my arm, to protect the play pages.

When I opened the door, he stood, smiling, with his belt in his hand.

He yanked me into the house, out of view of the neighbors.

"This isn't fair. My mother told me I could go!" I cried as he swung the belt.

Because I protested, he hit me for a long time. He grounded me for a month and forbade me to try out for the school play. I had work to do at home. I had to take the bus with everyone else.

I didn't care anymore what happened to me.

▲   ▲   ▲

It wasn't long after that I was invited by a classmate to go to a party. I barely knew her, and I didn't have a good feeling about her or the situation. But I wanted to go. I wanted to have some semblance of a normal teenage life.

I lied to my mother and said I was going to my friend's house to study for the evening. I didn't want to lie. How I wished that was truly what I was doing. My friend's boyfriend, who had been kicked out of high school, was waiting for us up the street in his busted-up car. We jumped in. A pair of fuzzy dice hung from the rearview mirror. I'd never been in a car with fuzzy dice.

No good can come from this, warned my knowing. *What does it matter if you lose face now by backing out? Ask them to drop you off. Now.*

I was still angry at my stepfather, and at my mother for

supporting him. Whatever happened, she took his side. She
didn't want to see what was really going on.

What good was it to know anything anyway? I argued at
the knowing. The more you knew, the more you endured.

My classmate pulled out beers hidden under her jacket.
We drank. Her older, slick-haired boyfriend drove us farther and farther out from the city, beyond my circle of
familiarity. The beer calmed my anxiety. Soon we were
at the lake, at a huge party. The music pounded. Drunken
strangers, mostly guys, surrounded me. I wanted to go
home, but I didn't want to go home at all. Hell, I reminded
myself, I had no home.

So I drank. The prickling anxiety that constantly
haunted me in my waking moments slid to my feet. The
more I drank, the more I didn't care that I couldn't sing in
the house anymore or try out for the play. I drank more to
fly above the rude story. I drank to obliterate my life.

My classmate and her boyfriend disappeared. They left
me alone without a ride home. I panicked. I had to find a
way back by my stepfather's curfew. If I were to show up
late and drunk, I feared I could be beaten to death.

I found a ride and paid for it without money. I had nothing else, and I was desperate and out-of-my-mind drunk. I
left part of myself behind.

▲   ▲   ▲

After that, I drank intermittently, usually on weekends.
I discovered that each kind of alcohol has its own spirit.
Drinking the sticky-sweet Southern Comfort associated
with the singer Janis Joplin evoked violence. The whiskey

was born in a New Orleans bar in 1874, in the wake of my people's removal. After I pulled down the front door of my apartment in my very early twenties, in a frustrated anger born of drinking Southern Comfort, I never drank it again.

Tequila was closer to its plant origins. I could see the agave plant at the edge of my consciousness. It was a medicine. I sensed the plant as a mothering being. It would bend over me to take care of me even as it would punish me, like a fierce, protective mother.

All of these plant medicines, like whiskey, tequila, and tobacco, are potent healers. There's a reason they're called spirits. You must use them very carefully. They open you up. If you abuse them, they can tear holes in your protective, spiritual covering.

▲　▲　▲

My stepfather began needling my mother to get rid of me. I was trouble, he said. I remember hugging myself under the blankets in the bedroom I shared with my sister as I overheard his plan to send me to a fundamentalist Christian school.

I had quit religion. He knew that to send me there would be the worst punishment.

Though I began attending the local Bible church after being lured to vacation Bible school in kindergarten, I stayed because I liked the treats. I grew to love Bible stories, and I hungered for God knowledge and loved the music. Church became an uneasy refuge from the chaos at home. Most of the children wouldn't sit with me in church, because I was Indian and my parents were divorced. There were kind people in the church community, like the family who for years drove my sister and me to church twice a week or more, without compensation for gas or time. Another parishioner, Mr. Hughes, carried bubblegum in the huge pockets of his big blue jacket. After church he passed out gum to all the children. He had a heart as huge as his pockets. We would have followed him anywhere, even without the bubblegum.

By the time I was thirteen I had grown tired of the misuse of the Bible to prove the superiority of white people, to enforce the domination of women by men, and I didn't agree with the prohibition on dancing and the warnings against prophecy and visions.

I decided to read the Bible through, searching to make my own sense of it. I read it through two or three times.

The Old Testament was basically tribal law for certain desert peoples in the Middle East. I found wisdom, poetry, and a great respect for dreams and visions. I also found no prohibition on dancing, which was proscribed by my church. King David danced before the altar. Women were as oppressed then as they were in Oklahoma.

Like the old-time powerful medicine people who spoke in metaphor, in poetry, Jesus Christ in the New Testament was an inspiration. He produced miracles and healed the people with words and deeds.

I delighted in scouring out shocking stories, like the one about Lot's daughters drugging him so he would sleep with them, to read to my mother from the Bible. "These stories can't be in the Bible!" she'd exclaim. And then I would point to the pages.

I often read to my mother. Once I read the opening to

Steinbeck's *Grapes of Wrath* to her. I thought she'd recognize her family's story, as she had grown up poor during the time of the Dust Bowl. She did. For several weeks she read the novel between jobs and while cooking for us.

One night, a month or so after my mother had started reading, she marched into my bedroom while I was getting ready for bed. She was furious with Steinbeck and me. Why had I given her a story to read that left the family broken down in the middle of the road? How could a writer abandon the characters and the story at a place of ruin? Unlike the reality we appeared to be living, she wanted her stories to have good endings.

I loved the erotic poetry of the Song of Solomon from the Bible. These were in essence love songs for a beloved. The beloved was also God. I turned to these songs in the Bible to escape the pedantic sermons of the preacher. I preferred to consider God as a beloved rather than as a wrathful white man who was ready to destroy anyone who had an imagination.

One Sunday morning a well-meaning member of the congregation brought a trio of young Mexican-American sisters to church. They sat together in the front row, next to their sponsor. I was immediately uneasy. I knew how difficult it had been for me being Indian in church, and they were darker Indian-looking girls. I had a bad feeling.

In the middle of the sermon the preacher breached protocol and called them out directly from the pulpit for whispering. It was all right to save dark-skinned souls at a distance, from Korea or Africa, but he made it clear that he did not want these people in his church.

The pastor continued to have difficulty concentrating

on his sermon. I watched as his face turned red from anger, and when he couldn't stand it any longer, he demanded that the girls leave. I watched with the rest of the congregation as the girls walked out of the church. I wanted to leave with them. I didn't have the courage to stand up with them and walk out. I never returned after that Sunday. From then on I suffered Sundays in a nervous silence in the house with my stepfather.

▲   ▲   ▲

We didn't live within walking or driving distance of a Creek church, nor did we have close relatives who would take us. My great-grandfather Henry Marcy Harjo had been a preacher, even a missionary to the Seminole Indians in Florida. Our great-grandfather Samuel Checotah was known as the first leader to convert to Christianity and became a Methodist minister. Because the tribe had out-lawed Christianity, he was beaten for his faith.

As my stepfather continued his scheme to send me to church school, I began making plans to run away. Like many others of my generation, I was attracted by the hippy migration to the Haight-Ashbury district of San Francisco. I liked all of it: the hip notion of love, the way people dressed, and the hippy anthems of acid-inspired music that tripped the airways. I had always felt different from oth-ers, and now here was a youthful tribe of people who were united in their statement of difference.

Love, love, love . . . was the opposite of living in a house with a man who stalked about looking for reasons to beat us. My stepfather had started coming to my room after my mother left for work early in the morning, while my sister still slept. I'd curl into my stomach and hold my breath as he rubbed my back. I was going to have to get out of there before anything else happened.

Once, not long after my stepfather and mother married, I came home from church to find my brothers and sister huddled together in fear in my room, waiting for me. They'd just watched from a crack in the door as our stepfather made our mother play Russian roulette with a loaded gun.

We never knew what he might do.

I researched bus costs. I asked about hitchhiking. A man I had met at a party said that if I could make it as far as San Francisco, he knew someone who could prostitute me. I didn't want to do that at all, but I was becoming desperate. If that was my only choice, I decided I would rather sell myself on the street than be imprisoned in a fundamentalist Christian school or surrender my body to my stepfather.

Though I was blurred with fear, I could still hear and feel the knowing. The knowing was my rudder, a shimmer of intelligent light, unerring in the midst of this destructive, terrible, and beautiful life. It is a strand of the divine, a pathway for the ancestors and teachers who love us.

My knowing told me that if I ran away, my life would turn even more chaotic. I saw my potential path as it ran from Tulsa to San Francisco. My lifeline was frayed and cut short.

As I pondered my dilemma as a teenager, curled up in my bed in the dark of night, I could feel the bright sun of knowing way in the distance, as if it were rising over the mountain of my distress. The sun gave me another way to consider God. The God I knew radiated such light. I could not accept an image of God as an angry white man who looked like my stepfather or the preacher.

The knowing told me there was another way. The knowing always spoke softly, wisely.

I told myself that the idea of running away should feel freeing, like flying, like hippies dancing in a love-in in a San Francisco park, but as I continued to consider it, I felt instead a heaviness, a terrible grief. I'd felt that kind of grief when I woke up from a dream of dying while giving birth on a South Pacific island.

In the dream I was in the story of a Polynesian girl. I speared food from the water. I loved the rhythm of the days. I remembered pig wrapped in banana leaves and cooked in an oven dug in the ground. I remembered how blue the ocean was. It was a blue rarely present now on Earth. I became pregnant. I had a premonition that the child and I would not survive. I went into labor, a labor that went on for more than two days. I died while giving birth. When I looked back as I turned toward the next world, I saw my exhausted rag of a body where I had cast it aside, and I saw the tiny body of my baby next to me.

At school I discovered information on opportunities for Indian students to go to Indian boarding school. I told my mother that I wanted to go to a school with other Indian students, a place where I would belong, where I would be normal. I wanted a smaller school, and I wanted to be far away from my stepfather. (I didn't tell her I wanted to escape my stepfather.)

My mother took me to the Okmulgee Agency of the

Bureau of Indian Affairs to apply. The personnel at the BIA office were kind and helpful. They knew my grandparents and spoke highly of my father's family and their contributions to our tribal society.

My mother and I began filling out the paperwork for me to attend the Chilocco Indian School. As we stood up at the end of the meeting with the agent, my mother mentioned my artwork. He then told us about the Institute of American Indian Arts. IAIA was a high school in Santa Fe, New Mexico, and included a two-year postgraduate program. Indian students from all over the country attended. He'd sent other Creek students there.

I felt brightness as he gave us a brochure and an application. I submitted original art to be considered, consisting of my fashion sketches and a cartoon series I created. I was accepted.

After that, I heard no more of church school.

That fall my mother and stepfather drove me to Santa Fe. I noticed a marked change in the quality of light when we made it to New Mexico. It lit up the mountains at dusk. I could feel the strength of my path and knew I was headed in the right direction. I felt inspired about my life in a way that I hadn't been since early childhood, when I used to go outside early in the morning to talk with the sun.

I was tremendously relieved to watch my stepfather pull away from the dorm, though I felt sad at my mother's leaving. I was concerned about her safety, but through the years she'd found a way to make a relatively safe road through the abyss of her husband's physical and psychological brutality.

▲   ▲   ▲

After I left for Indian school my brother Allen, who was next to me in age, was forced from the house. Instead of taking a regular high school academic track, he went to vo-tech to learn auto mechanics. When he was forced onto the street as a young teenager, at least he had a skill and could make a living.

My knowing showed my sister, Margaret, as protected from any advances from our stepfather. I could see that my youngest brother, Boyd, would be forced to leave the house like our brother.

A palm reader would tell me in the eighties that in the palm of my left hand exists an alternate lifeline. In that line was a girl of sixteen or seventeen. She was dead of a drug overdose on the street of a California city.

As I turned back into the dorm at dusk after I watched the family car leave, I knew I was turning toward home.

▲   ▲   ▲

When I started Indian school in Santa Fe in 1967, I was fresh from escaping the emotional winter of my childhood. I had been set free.

The famous Quapaw-Cherokee composer Louis Ballard was assigned as my adviser. Though I loved music and singing, I never took a class from him. I'd given up on music. In junior high, when the band teacher wouldn't allow me to play saxophone because I was female, I quit band. This happened at around the same time my stepfather forbade me to sing.

I spent hours hanging out with Ballard in his office

and studio. He was warm, affectionate, and liked having a young Oklahoma Creek around. He was like a father to me.

When I did return to music, after I was forty, Louis Ballard and I took up right where we had left off. I can still hear his voice urging me on in my creative musical efforts. Around five years ago he passed from this world. I spoke with him about a month before he moved on. He reiterated his belief in me, and I needed that belief. As we spoke, I saw him lifting up his feet and stepping over.

Music is direct communication with the sacred. It exists in a virtual invisible realm. There is no border of the corporeal, though words can be carried and lifted by music.

As adolescents we defined ourselves primarily by music. At Indian school we were either psychedelic visionaries with Jim Morrison and the Doors or Jimi Hendrix, or we were funky babies singing along with the Temptations, the Supremes, and the Four Tops. Or we danced Top Forty in white boots and bell-bottoms. If you were far, far out, you were a Frank Zappa freak. And then there were the country kings and queens with taped boots, up to the hats with attitude, waving them for Merle Haggard and Loretta Lynn. There were also powwow and traditional music practitioners.

Most of us crossed back and forth between these types of music, or thrived somewhere in the middle. I tended toward Zappa, jazz, Morrison, and funk. I went to every dance in the canteen and attended the larger light-show extravaganzas put on in the gym by the arts faculty and advanced students. The enigmatic painter and teacher Fritz

Scholder was one of the arts teachers who manipulated liquid gel projections for the light shows.

It was in the fires of creativity at the Institute of American Indian Arts that my spirit found a place to heal. I thrived with others who carried family and personal stories similar to my own. I belonged. Mine was no longer a solitary journey.

At Indian school we were Inupiat from Alaska, Seminole from Florida, and people from tribes from Oklahoma to Washington State. And though we were allied as young artists of a generation, we still contended with our tribal and historical differences. The Sioux students hung together. Their traditional enemies, the Pawnees, tended to avoid them, until they were paired as roommates or spent hours side-by-side making art in studio classes. Then those historical enmities fell away. Most joined with their traditional enemies when they were in the larger context of being a native arts student. All of us found commonality in creativity. I belonged to the "Civilized Tribes," which included the Creeks, Choctaws, Cherokees, Chickasaws, and Seminoles.

We were all "skins" traveling together in an age of metamorphosis, facing the same traumas from colonization and dehumanization. We were direct evidence of the struggle of our ancestors. We heard them and they spoke through us, though like others of our generation, we wore bell-bottoms and Lennon eyeglasses.

Santa Fe was at the epicenter of hippiedom in the West. Canyon Road was a trail of incense, psychedelic music, art, and a place where you could get turned on if you found the right person who didn't mind risking breaking the law by sharing with a minor. We were united by music, history, and art.

One of my classrooms was in a building originally constructed to teach "apartment living." There were stoves lined up along the wall. Previous generations of students had been taught housekeeping, farming, janitorial tasks, and other vocational skills. The students were trained to be low-paid labor for white families in the towns and cities. A fine arts program at that time would have been considered irrelevant and beyond the minds and talents of Indians.

As we made art, attended cultural events, and struggled with family and tribal legacies, we sensed that we were at the opening of an enormous indigenous cultural renaissance, poised at the edge of an explosion of ideas that would shape contemporary Indian art in the years to come. The energy crackled. It was enough to propel the lost children within us to start all over again. We honed ourselves on that energy, were tested by it, destroyed and recreated by it.

The Indian school world was rife with paradox. Formerly run like a military camp by the Bureau of Indian Affairs, the school had been transformed into a unique school for native arts, like the New York City *Fame* school but for Indian students. Almost overnight the staff, mostly established BIA employees, were asked to accommodate a fine arts curriculum and faculty—an assortment of idealistic and dedicated artists, both Indian and non-Indian.

We were given materials and encouraged to create, as we often did until three or four in the morning. Then we were awakened at exactly five-thirty A.M. by the dorm staff to report to details, jobs that included working in the kitchen and cleaning studios and offices. Then we went to our classes.

The most accomplished native and non-native artists taught our classes. Otellie Lolama, Hopi, taught traditional pottery; Fritz Scholder, Mission, taught painting; Allan Houser, Apache, taught sculpture; and Rolland Meinholtz, a Cherokee descendant, taught dramatic arts.

The academic classes were different. We had either stellar teachers who taught because they felt they could make a difference and loved what they were doing or those who signed on with the BIA because it was their last chance.

In one of my junior English classes we read aloud from fourth-grade readers. I always remember the story in that reader about a banker in a city in the Midwest who swept his sidewalk every morning before opening his bank. I looked around at our class. Many were gifted storytellers and speakers, but not in the English language. We were insulted and bored by the poor selection of materials. We could see that the teacher truly cared, but he didn't know what to do with a class of students with widely varying skills in the use of English.

Reading aloud is the last thing you'd ask a class of shy Indian students to do. It was a painful process. While the story was read word by word, student by student, the rest of us wrote notes and poems and sent drawings to each other. My poetry notes were rhymed doggerel, mostly rude commentary.

I was soon removed from class and sent to study solo with a young Jesuit priest who had come through town to visit the school before returning to Holy Rosary Mission in South Dakota. When the school urgently needed a teacher to fill in, he agreed and stayed over to teach through the spring.

As I walked into his classroom that first day, I was hidden in my navy pea coat and long dark hair that always clouded my face. Father-to-be John Staudenmaier saw into me and took care of my spirit. He gave me the freedom to read what I wanted. The only requirement was that I observe carefully and write about my observations. I read the poetry of Thomas Hardy and Emily Dickinson. I read O. Henry short stories.

I remember standing one night under the stars with him. I felt eternity running from the stars into us and between us. He was the first person to talk about the soul to me. He asked me to pay attention to the poetry of living.

In the spring the Preservation Hall Jazz Band came from New Orleans. They were on tour and played for us in an academic classroom. Because it was a Saturday afternoon, most of the students had checked out for the weekend or were in town. I was one of only three or four audience members to hear this renowned jamming band. The band blew us open with syncopated sound and soul. We could not stop smiling and moving.

▲   ▲   ▲

We continued to battle with troubled families and the history we could never leave behind. These tensions often erupted in violence provoked by alcohol, drugs, and the ordinary frustrations of being human.

One afternoon our drawing class was given an assignment to draw from nature. We scattered across campus to luxuriate in one of the first warm days of spring. I was intoxicated by the smell of the earth as it threw off heat, as I sat on the steps of the theater building with a few other students. We smoked cigarettes, sketched, and contemplated the afternoon. We were momentarily content.

Then one of our classmates ran by us. He leapt onto the hoods of every car in the administration parking lot, crushing in the roofs, one by one. He kicked in a set of windows lining the academic building. Around him a whirling halo glowed a brownish red. Within the whirlwind were racial slurs, his abandoned baby self, the running-away ghost of a father. Two teachers grabbed him and threw him to the ground.

Years later I thought of him as I drove through his reservation in South Dakota. I was impressed by the power that encircled his people. The gulf of discrepancy between the world of loss and the horses on the plains could be met only with anger.

Women often turn their anger inward, and at Indian school some of us mutilated ourselves. Each scar was evidence that we wanted to live. We had to keep knives away from one student. She was one of the best painting students. We carried another student to the Indian hospital to have her stomach pumped. She was a beautiful dancer from southern New Mexico. We had to hunt down another friend before she froze to death in the snow. She was trying to go home to a home that wasn't there in Montana.

One weekend some of my roommates decided to tattoo themselves with needles and black ink. I contemplated

what I would tattoo on my hands, but I was not enough
in love with anyone to tattoo his initials and L-O-V-E
on my knuckles, as one girl was doing. It was an initia-
tion of sorts, either for love or as a mark of blood, to show
bravery or to record a particular event, a breakup or an
accomplishment.

Years later I picked up my daughter from Indian school
near Gallup and met the boyfriend she was mourning
because they had to part for summer vacation. His hand
blazed with her initials carved in a heart. The cuts were still
weeping blood. I knew I had trouble.

I marked myself once with a knife. I was disappearing
into the adolescent sea of rage and destruction. The mark
of pain assured me of my own reality. The cut could speak.
It had a voice that cried out when I could not make a sound
in my defense. I never made such a mark again. Instead I
chose to slash art onto canvas, pencil marks onto paper, and
when I could no longer carry the burden of history, I found
other openings. I found stories.

This next story I found in my memory in a tangle of
Indian school stories. It is partially fictionalized.

*I thought of the old man as we huddled in the ditch
behind the dorms, passing around a bottle of sticky sweet
cherry vodka. Alcohol kept away the cold and the ghosts of
sadness, and after a few sips I was free to remember.*

*One night the moon was full, bright, with an aura of ice
as earth headed toward winter. It was in the time when our
father was still with us. He hadn't come home again, and
my mother waited up for him in front of the television, the*

blue flickering glow switching back and forth between light and dark.

The luminous road to the moon was strong and familiar as I made my way to the old man who was my guardian there. We did not need words to talk. That night he took me to a stone quarry, and we walked to the edge where the scrap pieces were piled together. Below it we could see the world I had come from. Across town, my father was coming out of Cain's Ballroom with a blond woman on his arm. They were kissing and laughing. We could see my mother doze as the television screen blurred, and then the baby awakened and she went to him, changed his diaper, and held him close to her neck as she turned on the light in the kitchen to make his bottle.

This was the first time we had come to this place together. I knew then that it would be a very long time before I would see the old man again, and I felt sad. We watched the story below us as it unwound through time and space, unraveling like my mother's spools of threads when she accidentally dropped them. But I would not recall any of it for years.

When I returned to my body at dawn, my father showed up at home with smeared lipstick on his white shirt and the terrible anger of a trapped cat inside him.

I watched the moon from a distance. It was a slender knife in the winter sky. I hoped the old man couldn't see me sitting drunk here, beneath his home in the moon.

I had to keep from staring at the new student, Lupita. Her perfect skin was café au lait, and her black eyes were elegant like a cat's. She announced that the first thing she had done when she arrived at school was check out the male population and she was going to give a report. We laughed and leaned forward to listen.

"What's the name of that Sioux guy who paints large canvases with the geometric designs? With the nice smile and perfect back, always running touchdowns between classes?"

"John Her Many Horses," we chimed. Every girl on campus had noticed him.

"Now that morsel over there . . ." She motioned to Herbie Nez. He was Navajo and as slim as a girl.

"He's much too pretty. I could eat him up in one bite," she teased.

Herbie's hearing was like a finely cut crystal and tuned into everything, even the songs and cries of spirits who hung around the school. He could hear the cries of children dragged in the early years to the school against their will.

Herbie looked over at us and batted his eyelashes. We all laughed together and downed the next round. Then suddenly our party was over. The dorm patrol surprised us in the nearly moonless night. We scattered across the grounds into the dark to save ourselves from detention, restriction, and being sent back home.

I ran until I couldn't run anymore. By the time I made it back to our room, my roommate had already been caught, tried, and judged and was packing her bags to go home. She was the first that semester to be kicked out of school for drinking. She was to be the object lesson for all of us.

Her family came after breakfast the next morning, just as a light rain blew in over the mountains. We all watched apprehensively from the dorm living room as her father stiffly lifted her suitcases into their truck to take her back to the reservation. When she climbed in next to her mother and brothers and sisters, she turned and waved a heavy goodbye.

That night Georgette Romero woke up the whole dorm. First I heard screams and then footsteps running down the hall toward my room, which was in the farthest wing. Lupita saw everything, she told me later, because she was up writing a letter to her mother at four in the morning. When Georgette ran by, Lupita saw her being chased by a ghost. Her Apache roommates refused to let her back into their room and burned cedar to dispel the evil. They didn't want a girl with a ghost in their room, and neither did anyone else. My room had an extra bed, and it was decided that she would move to my room. That night and for many nights after, I stayed alert in the dark and didn't sleep, anticipating the ghost's return.

Georgette's books were all over the floor. Her plastic beauty case overflowed with makeup and polishes, flooding the counter over the drawers that we were supposed to share. For hours she scraped and rubbed off chipped polish on her nails, then reapplied numerous thick coats, smelling up the room with polish and acetone. She left used dabs of cotton and underwear scattered on the floor. At first I was amused by this alien creature, and told myself that she had made herself her own canvas. But she was getting on my nerves. I spent more and more time in the painting studio or sat on the fire escape, listening to music.

One afternoon when I came back to my room from classes, I couldn't hear anything for the whine blasting from Georgette's favorite country station. I had just been summoned to meet with the head dorm matron, Mrs. Wilhelm, in half an hour, and after the bare escape I had every reason to be concerned. I had to make a plan about what I would do, where I would run if I got kicked out.

"Hey, I need that!" Georgette gestured to me with her nail polish applicator as I turned down the volume, almost muting it. "I had a rough day."

"Peace," I said, and made the peace sign with my fingers. I turned up the music a notch, then opened the windows to let in some air. I took a deep breath to relieve my panic. I had to get my thoughts straight before going into the meeting with the dorm matron. I had to have a plan.

I couldn't go back to my family, I would tell her. I would kill myself first.

I thought about killing myself. Once when the pressure was too much, when the stepfather was bearing down on me, I sneaked a kitchen knife into my bed. I cut myself on the wrist. The cut was superficial. None of our knives were sharp. But the cut temporarily relieved the pressure. I felt calm. Then my mother came into the room, brought there by mother instinct. She lifted my blanket and saw the knife and my cut. Pain broke her face. I never tried it again. When I thought about it, I'd see her face guarding me.

Across the way, in the boys' dorm, I could hear Herbie practicing his guitar. We shared a love for jazz, Jimi Hendrix, and esoteric philosophies.

"Our dark sides are compatible," I told him one night as we flew with Jimi's guitar, far from the dancers we could hear in the distance practicing in the gym, far from the school, from pain, high on smoke, sitting on the floor of his dorm room.

"Hmmmmmm," he answered. "True as horses running across mesas, breathing clouds."

"*Perfect,*" I answered.

And then we laughed. Though he was born in a hogan and didn't speak English until he was sent to a Catholic boarding school, and I was born in a city speaking English, we fit. My father's tribal language was a secret used by his relatives, who didn't like my mother because she came from a poor family. My father's relatives and ancestors were tribal leaders, beauty queens, and artists. My mother's relatives were musicians and storytellers and didn't like to hold nine-to-five jobs. My parents were from enemy tribes, which set up a conflict in my blood.

Herbie's spirit gleamed and spun and called to me to climb higher and higher. We flew, and all the weight of fear and doubt fell away.

Georgette was in love with Clarence, Herbie's cousin from the other side of the Navajo reservation. Clarence was one of those shy-eyed Navajo men with big eyelashes and a tight, tapered back. He lived for rodeo, for horses, bulls, and girls. Georgette's moods fluctuated according to her sightings of Clarence. He was her sole focus and the reason for her beauty tricks.

"So did Clarence ask you to marry him today?" I joked.

Georgette glared at me. "That Mexican girl better go back where she came from, is all I can say," she snapped. She was talking about Lupita.

"You mean the opera singer," I answered. Lupita wanted to be an opera singer, went the rumor, but the idea of any of us becoming an opera singer seemed preposterous. It was wildly possible, just not likely. Most of us girls would most likely move home, have babies, and do art at the kitchen table.

Partying in the ditch the previous weekend, Lupita hadn't

looked like an opera singer; she was one of us. I could still hear her laugh as we ran through the dark from the dorm police. It was a trained laugh—and for a moment I could imagine her as an opera singer, far away from here, on a stage where her talent and shine could amount to something. She was half Mexican, and her father was from a tribe in Oregon I had never heard of until I came here to school. The word was, this school was her last chance.

Herbie told me that Clarence had made a bet he could have Lupita within a week. She would be easy. All the boys were watching to see what would happen and were placing bets.

"Did you place a bet?" I asked Herbie.

"No way," he answered. "But I'm placing a bet that I'll have that Lewis wrapped around my finger by Saturday night."

"Yes, the most improbable candidate for your love in the whole school."

"I like a challenge," he said.

We laughed at the incongruity. Lewis was Clarence's best friend. He rode bulls and even looked like a bull. He was square to the earth and thought of himself as a stud. He would beat Herbie up if he caught Herbie staring at him in public.

Lupita's singing pulled me up the hallway as I walked to my meeting with Mrs. Wilhelm. Her office was near the dorm entrance, where Lupita now perched, a crowd around her. I stopped to listen along with everyone else who was captured by her voice. Her voice was a living, breathing thing, like Jimi Hendrix's guitar, like Jackson Pollock's paintings.

My father had told me that some voices are so true they

can be used as weapons, can maneuver the weather and change time. He said that a voice that powerful could walk away from the singer if it is shamed. After my father left us, I learned that some voices could deceive you. There is a top layer and there is a bottom layer, and sometimes they don't match. My stepfather's voice had a top layer. It was jovial and witty and knew how to appeal to women. The bottom layer was a belt studded with anger.

Everyone clapped when the song was over.

"Forget opera," I blurted out. "You can sing anything you want." Everyone turned to look at me, including Clarence, who was leaning against the wall, pretending he was an innocent audience member.

"Hey, thanks," Lupita said warmly. "Do I know you?"

We had met at the ditch. Maybe she had forgotten, and then I saw her eyes move sideways toward the dorm assistants, who were listening to everything. We couldn't be too careful. Maybe she too was waiting for Mrs. Wilhelm.

"I'm Lupita, from the planet Venus." She smiled at me, aware of the rapt attention of the high school boys, who all snickered when she mentioned Venus.

I introduced myself as being from Oklahoma and added, "Oklahoma is a long way from Venus." Everyone laughed. We were all in awe of this girl with the magic voice whose easy sexual suggestiveness reminded us of an earthy goddess. Though she was my age, Lupita seemed suddenly older as she slid her hands along her tight sheath skirt. Her nails were long and manicured, the look Georgette strived for but would never get. In that small moment I felt sorry for Georgette. She didn't have a chance.

"Do you really like my singing?"

She glanced over at Clarence, who gave her a shy dance of his eyes. It was obvious that despite his bet, they had a thing for each other. There was a light that jumped between them, an electrical force so strong that it sparkled in the late afternoon sun. Who was after whom? I wondered.

"Lupita, can you move your admiration society outside?"

It was Mrs. Wilhelm. I had briefly forgotten about her. She motioned me into her office with her determined German chin and sharp gray eyes. Suddenly I was afraid again. The door shut with a precise click. She motioned me to sit at the table I had shined with lemon wax just that morning. My work detail was to clean her office after breakfast before I went to class. I did so diligently, with respect and fear.

"I have something I want to show you," Mrs. Wilhelm said. Here it is, I thought. I expected her to pull out the weekend's report on the ditch episode, or at least to point out an uneven wax job. Instead she put a letter in front of me.

It was addressed to her, and it was from my stepfather. I had no idea why my stepfather would write to Mrs. Wilhelm or any administrator at the school. I had never seen him write a letter to anyone. His routine was to come in from work at four, find a reason to hit my brothers or me, then open and read the evening paper. My mother would hide in the kitchen cooking dinner, though she was tired after waitressing all day at the diner for the old lady from back East who ran the place.

One time I lost it. My mother was exhausted from working a double shift. My stepfather sat in his huge chair barking out orders. He yelled at my mother to cut his meat, to bring him *another glass of iced tea. Then he snapped at her because she wasn't moving fast enough.*

"Hurry up, bring me some more ice! What's taking you so long?" He had just asked her for something at the other end of the house a few minutes before.

I had to say something.

"Why don't you buy her a pair of roller skates so she can get around faster?"

I was belted. I was grounded forever. But it was worth it.

The envelope had been opened neatly by Mrs. Wilhelm with the electric letter opener I dusted every morning. I took out the letter. He had used my mother's drugstore stationery and had written with blue ink.

> *Dear Mrs. Wilhelm,*
>
> *I am writing to you because I think there are some things you need to know about our daughter who is now a student at your school. We had quite a problem with her when she was in our home and could not control her. Watch out for her. She will steal. She is not to be trusted.*

I was not his daughter—I had never heard him call me that—nor had I stolen anything. Tears threatened, but I refused to give him that satisfaction, even if he was six hundred miles away. My face blushed; I was stung by his betrayal. He was the one who had stolen: he had stolen my mother's life and was attempting to steal my reputation. I stuttered, but nothing came out.

"This is what I think about this letter," Mrs. Wilhelm told me. She tore it into pieces and threw them in the trash can. I was both relieved and surprised. I had never believed it possible to be trusted over the word of a white man who

*belonged to the Elks. As I left her office, I promised myself
that I would never drink again. Mrs. Wilhelm had believed
in me. She had given me another chance.*

*I walked into my room after the meeting to find Lupita
sitting on my bed while Georgette struggled to pull on my
prized fake suede hip-hugger bell-bottoms. They were stuck
at her hips. Everyone on our floor shared clothes, though they
usually asked permission first. Georgette hadn't asked.*

*"Excuse me!" I shouted over the radio just as she trium-
phantly snapped the top button.*

*"They fit," Georgette said. She pushed a chair up to the
dresser mirror and climbed up to admire herself front and back.
"Do you mind if I borrow them?"*

*Lupita was absentmindedly sifting through Georgette's
box of polishes.*

"Aren't they a little tight?" I asked.

"No, they fit perfectly."

*For the sake of making friends with Lupita, I momen-
tarily let it go, wincing as I watched Georgette make furtive
dance movements as she watched herself in the mirror.*

*"Be careful," I warned her as she hopped down from her
pedestal. "Those are my favorite pants."*

*Lupita's kind of talent was rare and burned bright. The
school saw this and was paying for private music lessons, she
told us as Georgette picked through nail polishes and pulled
out what I thought was a horrible color for Lupita. Lupita
humored her, but I could see that she was no fool.*

*The music teacher wasn't just teaching her to sing. She
laughed as she told us about his wandering hands when he
put his arms around her to demonstrate abdominal breathing.*

"So where is your mother from?" I figured I might as well

find out the answer directly. Lupita's stories about being from Venus, her outrageous flirting, and her sudden appearance in the middle of the semester made her a target for rumors. Not only had I heard that this school was her last chance, but there was speculation on her mother's absence.

"Venus," she said.

She was serious. Her claim was not just a flirting device to attract boys. She had to believe this so she wouldn't fall apart.

It was then I remembered the old man and how I used to fly to the moon. I remembered the stone quarry and my mother holding the baby. I remembered my father. I felt lonesome, my stomach scraped by the edge of sorrow.

Lupita opened up and we talked about everything—about our fathers, about the ability to fly in dreams. Georgette listened quietly as she polished Lupita's nails. I told Lupita I wanted to paint, to be an artist. She told me that what she wanted was someone to love her. And then she said to me nonchalantly, as she looked sideways at Georgette, "What do you know about that Navajo boy, the cowboy with the eyelashes—Clarence?" She had perfect timing, the mark of a good hunter or singer. Then she said directly to Georgette, "He's a good kisser."

I hated confrontation and kept quiet.

"He's spoken for," spit Georgette, who stood up quickly to face Lupita, spilling acetone all over her and my prized suede pants. The whole room stank of rotten apples.

Lupita knew exactly what Georgette had been up to all along when she invited her to our room. I wondered if she knew anything about Clarence's bet and whether I should tell her, and if so, when. Lupita picked up Georgette's sharp nail file and began to file her nails.

Georgette wasn't through, though.

"You Mexican bitch!" she snapped. "Get out of here."

"This is my room too," I said. "She can stay. And by the way, please take off my pants."

Georgette glared at me as she quickly replaced my pants with her skirt. She kicked the ruined pants aside.

"You're both sick," she spit out. "Nobody can be from Venus or anyplace else but here."

She marched out of the room carrying her case of nail polish and a story she would vent to her friends in the next room.

Later I set out for the painting studio to get myself back together. When I painted, everything went away: the seductions, the sad need for attention, the missing fathers, fearful mothers, and evil stepfathers. I could fly to the moon, and to Venus too, if I wanted. I understood Lupita when she said she was from Venus. I was also from somewhere far away, the other side of the Milky Way, and would return there someday. I knew it, as I knew I could count on cerulean blue to be absolutely cerulean blue when I spread it on a canvas.

An approaching cold front froze the stars to the dark sky. The Powwow Club was practicing in the gym, and a song flew out the tall narrow windows toward the white shell of the moon. The moon leaned delicately toward the bright point of Venus, framed by the graceful cottonwoods lining the sidewalk. I felt flawed, imperfect, but what haunted me was not flamboyant like Georgette's ghost. It was a subtle thing, a delicate force, like the field of stars under the sky when we danced in the summer. I was haunted by a paradox: if there is such beauty, then why are we suffering?

As I opened the door to the studio, Herbie jumped me. I screamed. I chased him, then held him down, made him

promise never to frighten me again. Then I told him every-
thing: about Lupita, about Georgette, about Mrs. Wilhelm
and my stepfather, about the moon. He walked around me as
I talked and got out my paints. He was high on possibilities,
on hope, beer, and smoke. He reminded me that he had come
over to take me to the dance at the canteen.

"No!" I told him. "No, I can't. Today I made a promise
to myself, and I can't risk getting sent home. I need to paint."

The incantations of the Doors wound through the campus
and through the door of the studio, tempting me.

"You're running away from yourself," he said. "You're
hiding from reality. Let's go! Besides, I need you for courage
to check somebody out for me. Aieeeee."

I knew he meant Lewis. And when I thought of Lewis, I
remembered Lupita and the deal Clarence had going. Tonight
was the deadline. I had to find Lupita and warn her before
it was too late.

The canteen was jammed. Herbie immediately pulled me
out onto the dance floor. Dancing was like painting, like fly-
ing. Through rhythm I could travel toward the stars. Herbie
and I could stay on the dance floor for hours, and if we stayed
in the canteen and danced I couldn't drink or get into any
other kind of trouble. While we danced I kept my eyes on
the door, looking for Lupita. We danced every dance until a
Mexican song interrupted us and all the Apache girls flooded
the dance floor.

While they weaved back and forth to the bright music of
the ranchero, Herbie bought us Cokes, and I looked around
the room for Lupita. I didn't see her anywhere. I didn't see
Clarence either. Georgette stood outside the glass doors of the

entrance. She was small and alone. I watched her ask to borrow a cigarette from another student. She lit it. I remembered the night she upset the whole dorm with her panicked run from the ghost chasing her, and the big stink her roommates had caused when they demanded she move from their room. I felt sorry for the girl with the scratchy army blanket draped over her shoulders. The ghost had not reappeared, but the fear followed her.

I spotted Clarence coming up out of the dark, from the direction of the ditch. He was smiling and laughing too hard, walking with Lewis. Lupita wasn't with them. Clarence grabbed Georgette a little roughly. She smiled and melted into him, and then they came through the door and onto the dance floor, Lewis following behind them. Georgette beamed and made sure I saw her.

"Where's Lupita?" I demanded. A knot formed in my stomach. Georgette glared at me.

"She's on Venus," said Clarence, and he and Lewis laughed. I didn't like the sound of their sly laughter.

I pulled a reluctant Herbie behind me. "We have to look for Lupita," I urged. He slid out the door of the packed canteen with me.

"Wait, wait," he protested as he stared back at Lewis, who had no idea Herbie was interested in him. But Herbie knew better than to reveal his attraction, and pantomimed his broken heart behind Lewis's broad back.

We found Lupita almost immediately. "Over here," she called brightly. She waved us into the shadow between the painting and drawing studios, where she was alone.

"Okay, Venus," joked Herbie. "This better be good. I just left the man of my dreams to come and look for you."

Her eyes shined as she pulled a pint of Everclear from under her jacket.

"You guys go ahead," I said. "I'll sit this one out."

I was trying to be good. It was then that I saw the rough smudge of dirt on Lupita's jacket, the dainty lace of twigs on her thick black hair, and the bruise decorating her wrist. I thought of Clarence and Lewis walking smugly into the dance. I knew they'd had their way with her. It was more than I could bear. I took a drink, then another.

I lost track of time. One minute we were all back in the canteen dancing in a line to "Cotton-Eyed Joe" and then the next we were sitting under the moon out near the ditch with a stranger from town we'd hired to make a liquor run for us. The earth was spinning, and we were spinning with it. We leaned into the burn. Lupita told us about her life, about how her mother had died when she was ten years old and left her with her father. She told how her father would tie her hair up every morning with her mother's ribbons before they left to work the fields together.

Herbie showed us the scar on his back made by a man who beat him and then raped him for his girlish ways. He made it sound funny, but I didn't laugh. I didn't say anything: I was numb and flying far away, listening to the whir of the story as it unwound beneath the glowing moon.

Herbie disappeared somewhere in the dark, and I could hear him throwing up. Someone was singing round-dance songs. A dog barked far, far away. Lupita had drifted into the bushes for what seemed years when the warning bell sounded from the girls' dorm. The sky was still spinning, but I willed myself to walk, step by step, to find Lupita, to make it back to the dorm in time. I looked for her through the blur of stars and sadness. I lost her.

Without warning I remembered the stacked stones in the quarry on the moon. I saw the unraveling story as it spun through time and space. And I saw what the old man had shown me that I hadn't been able to recall until now—how each thought and action fueled the momentum of the story, how vulnerable we were to forgetting, all of us.

The final bell rang and I barely made it to my room, where I summoned a bit of soberness to save my life. I brushed my teeth so I wouldn't smell like a drunk.

"Breathe," said the dorm assistant, whose job it was on Friday and Saturday nights to go to each room and smell each girl's breath for alcohol. She stood poised with her pen, ready to make a mark against my name. I admired her clean life. Her parents showed up every weekend to take her home, and returned her with chili and fresh bread. She stayed on the safe side of rules. I breathed. Then breathed again easily when she marked me present and sober.

No one had seen Lupita. Georgette floated into our room. "By the way," she said coolly, "Mrs. Wilhelm is looking for you. She wants you to come to her office."

I was still drunk when I entered Mrs. Wilhelm's office, though I had learned to hide it. Lupita was sobbing. Mrs. Wilhelm looked disappointed.

"I want to go home. I want to go back to Venus," Lupita cried as she buried her face in her arms.

I had failed to warn her in time, and I had failed the trust of Mrs. Wilhelm, who was the only person who had ever stood with me against the lies of my stepfather. Now Lupita *would get sent home, not to Venus but to the father who had been sleeping with her since she was ten.*

"Were you with Lupita tonight?" Mrs. Wilhelm asked me.

Immediately I thought of Georgette, the snitch. But I knew that wasn't really what mattered. The truth was a path clearer than anything else, a shining luminous bridge past all human failures. I could see the old man on the moon who always demanded nothing less.

"Yes, I was with Lupita," I confessed.

I knew I was most likely dooming myself to the house of my stepfather.

"Go take care of her," Mrs. Wilhelm said. "I will talk with the two of you tomorrow when you're sober." Then she slapped each of us with a month of restriction. "I need you here so I can keep a closer eye on you," she said.

I led Lupita back to her room. All night I held her while she cried for her mother, for home, all night, as we flew through the stars to the planet Venus.

WEST

West is the direction of endings. It is the doorway to the ancestors, the direction of tests. It represents leaving and being left and learning to find the road in the darkness.

One night as I raced down the sidewalk at Indian school to a dance at the canteen, I accidentally ran smack into an older Cherokee student and fell. He helped me hobble over to the porch of the boys' dorm. He was on his way to party with the over-twenty-ones. There were several older students at the school in the postgraduate program. He had that easy and familiar humor of Oklahoma Indians. I felt at home in his voice and with his teasing.

"Cat got your tongue?" he said.

I kept my head down, and my hair was a curtain covering half my face. My knees were just scraped.

"Looks like you'll live," he said, laughing.

I smiled.

He helped me up and ditched his party to go with me to the dance. We discovered that we were both James Brown freaks, and when we danced, we got off the dance floor only for him to take a smoke break. We talked about our plans to be artists, about our families. He was Cherokee and familiar like my relatives and neighbors.

"My father is Creek," I told him as he cupped his hand around a match to steady the flame before lighting up. I built my father up as a descendant of warriors, when he was running around somewhere south of Okmulgee with a different woman every night.

His parents were both Cherokee. His father was mixed with German. His mother was full-blooded and had been adopted by another full-blood family in Tahlequah when her parents died not long after she was born. Many of our people died young of tuberculosis and other diseases that took root from loss. We discovered that our mothers were probably distantly related on the Cherokee side.

His first memory, he told me that night as we continued to talk under a night sky rich with falling stars, was of a boy with burned skin being brought to his grandfather for a healing. The skin was flayed over the boy's face in waves. He watched as his grandfather sang and prayed, then took water in his mouth and spat on the burn. He did this many times. The boy and the boy's father returned two weeks later with some bags of groceries and a wood carving in gratitude for the healing. There was no sign or mark of the burn on the boy's body.

"My story is like a falling star," I said as we watched a small universe blaze and fall from the sky. "That star was a person. It was a being of fire that laughed and cried. Someone is missing that star in the sky. The star's lover is bereft, calling its name."

As I spoke, I realized that I did not want to be alone beneath the eternal sweep of the sky. His eyes told me, neither did he. He took my hand and pulled me close against him. I liked his earthy smell, his muscular definition. We became lovers. I was sixteen.

▲   ▲   ▲

I got involved with the school theater program as a production assistant for our fall school production of Shelagh Delaney's *A Taste of Honey*. I enjoyed being part of the process of the play as it unfolded from a few pages in a thin book of poetic, dramatic storytelling, with characters who were much like us, to the building of lights, sets, blocking, acting, and the culmination to opening night, where the magic was let loose. Our drama coach, Rolland Meinholtz, was a master teacher. He expected us to be professional, and we responded in like manner. He was one of the first people to teach me this foundation principle in the art of teaching.

I wasn't a theater major, nor did I take any music or creative writing classes. I was fully ensconced in 2-D arts, taking drawing and painting classes.

I'll never forget hanging with a friend on the steps of our dorm as we filled out our elective choices for spring semester. I remember her urging me to sign up for an acting class with her. She was dramatic and extroverted, so that made sense to me, for her. I felt I was more suited to bending close to canvas and finding the path through color and design.

"No," I told her. "I will never get on a stage."

Yet I went ahead and scribbled out my previous choice and wrote in "acting." In retrospect I believe the knowing was directly involved in this change. It was not my conscious choice.

I learned that acting was not just looking pretty or acting dramatically onstage. It demanded an alert and knowing body with powerfully developed links to the subconscious. We took two hours of modern dance in the afternoon under the direction of the Blackfeet dancer and choreographer Rosalie Jones. With Meinholtz we learned storytelling, stagecraft, and lighting. We meditated. We tapped into the deep psychological stores within us. I began to discover that rooms of knowing existed throughout our bodies.

When I was there, in the midst of each of these activities, I felt truly me. Theater gave me a door through which to enter the dreaming realm. I soon had a lead in a play written by Monica Charles, one of the older students. She was Klamath Indian from the Pacific Northwest. Her play, *Mowitch*, was part of a show of plays and dances in what would be called the "Deep Roots, Tall Cedar" show. My boyfriend also had a role, and began to emerge in dance classes with a tremendous gift. Later in reviews he would be compared to Rudolf Nureyev and offered dance scholarships back East.

We began rehearsals in earnest, as a tour was set up for the Pacific Northwest. I was one of only two high school students. The second was Marcus Garcia, from Santo Domingo Pueblo. He and I were moved to dorms with older students, and our schedules were shifted to accommodate our long and late rehearsals, which often went until two or three in the morning. Under the direction of our visionary director, our company of intense, creative, and often troubled teenagers had become a professional-seeming troupe of dancers and actors with a unique, contemporary indigenous aesthetic. The comedian Jonathan Winters heard about us and was an enthusiastic supporter, and the dancer José Limón flew in from New York to witness our ceremonial dance plays.

When the letters for permission to go on tour went to our parents, my stepfather denied permission. He gave no reason for his denial.

Because of my stepfather's strange behavior, school officials read his actions as abuse. Years later one of the staff members told me that the administration had begun steps to put me in the custody of the school.

The director called my mother. She agreed to sign the release so I could go on the professional tour. For the first time since she had married our stepfather, she came through for me. My stepfather quit speaking to her, and didn't speak to her for months.

The tour remains a highlight of my life. We performed and gave workshops on the Swinomish Reservation in La Conner, Washington; we performed in the theater beneath the Space Needle in Seattle; we performed at Monica Charles's reservation on the peninsula of Washington State, where we got to meet her uncle, who was the inspiration for *Mowitch;* then we drove to La Grande, Oregon, and put on workshops and performed. We were surprised when residents drove up beside us as we walked along the road in La Grande and threw rocks and yelled "Dirty Indians" at us. They told us to get out of town. They didn't want Indians.

Most of all I remember the troupe as a creative, coherent family. Each of us was young, with tremendous personal, familial, and historical dysfunctions and gifts. We pulled together to create groundbreaking art that inspired.

After the tour, some of us left for college or headed to New York City to take drama workshops and look for acting jobs. One joined the army. Others headed back to the reservation to create art. I returned to the house of my stepfather, secretly pregnant by my Cherokee boyfriend and with no plans, no idea at all as to where I was going or how I was going to get there.

▲   ▲   ▲

When we parted ways after the tour, the baby's father promised he'd send a bus ticket for me to Tahlequah, in Cherokee
lands, where he was living with his mother and daughter.
I made sure I was the first to the mailbox every afternoon
to check for the ticket. I was four months pregnant. I was
beginning to show and hid my stomach under large shirts.
I could not snap or button my pants underneath.

I told my mother that I was getting married, that my
husband-to-be was sending for me. I was not yet eighteen
years old. Eighteen was the legal age for marriage in the
state of Oklahoma. My mother must have known that fact,
but she asked me no questions. I recognized that it would
be a relief to get me out of the house. I was the cause of
the tension.

After two weeks, when there was no letter or bus ticket,
I asked my brother Allen for the money to get to Tahlequah. Allen always had money. Once I had to break up a
sweatshop he had going with our sister, Margaret. He hired
her to weave cheap loop potholders for a nickel apiece, then
sold them for a dollar each. I told her she should charge
more and she quit. He soon found another way to make
money. He needed it for all of his bike and race projects.
He was brilliant with his ongoing constructions, which
included upside-down bikes and fast go-carts hammered
together with found items. He and I sold white paper
bags of Daylight Doughnuts door-to-door in Skiatook,
Oklahoma. The shop's owner would sip coffee and read
his paper in his car as my brother and I sold to women in
housecoats, men who were already downing their morning

beer, and families watching Saturday-morning cartoons. I spent my money on photography. I bought film and paid for development. I also bought art supplies and fabric to make clothes.

Allen and I covered for each other. I never told our mother of the time he hot-wired a huge yellow earthmover parked at the church down the street. He took it on a joy-ride through the neighborhood while she was at work. He must have been only ten or eleven years old.

My brother loaned me the money, and I bought my bus ticket and told my mother that my boyfriend had sent for me. When the bus left from the Tulsa Greyhound station, everything I owned fit in my army-surplus Indian school footlocker. I left with about ten dollars in cash.

As Tulsa, the city of my birth, fell behind me, I barely noticed the landscape while the bus navigated the country two-lanes that carried me toward an uncertain future. I imagined what would happen when I arrived at the bus station in Tahlequah. He would be there to greet me. I would go with him. Somewhere. I knew he was living with his mother, and she was taking care of his young sister, who was still in elementary school, and his daughter, Ratonia, a two-year-old. His mother knew nothing of me.

I pulled out the photograph he'd given me at Indian school of his daughter, taken the summer before. Squinting her eyes at the sun was a wiry and energetic one-and-a-half-year-old who, with her Cherokee nose and smiling eyes, resembled her father, the man I loved.

His daughter's mother was my age when they got pregnant. They were living in Oregon, where his mother worked in a clinic. He had heard that his baby's mother was drinking. He went to her house and found a party going on. His daughter was wrapped in blankets on the floor and could have been stepped on, he said, so he picked her up and fled with her and his mother back to Oklahoma.

I thought to myself when I heard the story, *I guess it's all right for him to party because he's a man. And he had his mother to take care of the baby.*

In the black-and-white photograph of his daughter, small frame houses were in the background. I determined that if he was not at the bus station to meet me, I would try to locate his mother's house from the photograph. To find it would be difficult, as all the houses looked the same.

What if I could not find the house? What if I did find him and he refused to help or denied he knew me?

He met me at the bus station, giving no explanation about not writing or not having sent for me, or about the lack of a bus ticket. We immediately pawned my turquoise ring for food.

▲   ▲   ▲

He put me up temporarily in the living room of two of his friends. The house was filthy, with stacks of dishes and uneaten food and piles of clothes through the place. I cleaned. He brought his daughter over to me every morning for child care. She was inquisitive, talkative, and ever hyper. She could not stop moving—opened every drawer, every closet, pulling everything out. The first day she unlatched the screen door and ran down the street, laughing as I chased her.

That living arrangement was for just a week.

My husband-to-be was concerned about his mother finding out about me. He next attempted to hide me by putting me up at his grandmother's house and staying there with me at night. But it is impossible to hide a pregnant woman, or anybody else, in a close Indian community in which everyone knows everyone else's business, or thinks they do. Word got out, especially after I was seen sitting in the town square with his grandmother, who spent the crisp mornings with her friends under the eaves of the old bandstand. I enjoyed that time with them. They were the heart of the nation and made note of the current state of affairs as they watched people enter and leave the bank and the various establishments and agencies around the square. They didn't say much, and I didn't understand much of their Cherokee. To be included in this daily meeting under the oak trees gave me a fresh peace that was rare everywhere else.

Once when my boyfriend's grandmother got her monthly check we ate lunch at the diner across the street. I watched her unclasp her black patent leather bag and empty the basket of crackers into it to take home. I tried to duck, but my growing belly made it impossible. I bumped and spilled my glass of water, which called even more attention to us. She, however, had grace as she carefully left change for a tip, and we walked back to her house.

Soon thereafter I was summoned to my soon-to-be mother-in-law's house. I was nervous. I had been warned by anyone who could take me aside that she was jealous, overprotective, and mean. They were right. What they didn't say was how attractive she was, how she was still in good form despite the rough years, her dark hair thick and lightly curled. It was her dark eyes that told the other story. They took in the edges of things, the tatters, and left the good behind.

My lively new daughter ran up to us as soon as she saw us. My new sister-in-law quietly drew pictures of horses at the table.

I moved in with the family in my mother-in-law-to-be's tiny one-bedroom house that afternoon, because, as she told her son, "You can't stay there and live off your grandmother." That much was true. But she also wanted to think she had some control of the gossip. If I was in her house, she would know my whereabouts and could be the authority. She was also pragmatic: I could watch the children.

I adjusted. I had no choice.

I hated the days when she was moody and critical. I could smell those days coming from far off, like the ozone in a storm front. She might start with "Why aren't you with your mother?" meaning, why doesn't your mother take care of you? She reproached me as I washed dishes after eating food bought with her hard-earned money. Or she would say, "Your mother is rich. Why can't she send us money?" She assumed my mother was rich because she was a lighter-skinned Cherokee who passed for white and lived in Tulsa. I promised myself that as soon as the baby was born we would find our own place. I would swallow hard. I didn't like being at the mercy of someone else's kindness. I did everything I could to make myself useful around the house. "My mother isn't rich," I answered.

During my last visit to the clinic at the Indian hospital I was given the option of being sterilized. It was explained to me that the moment of birth was the best time. I was handed the form but chose not to sign. I didn't think much of it at the time. Many Indian women who weren't fluent in English signed, thinking it was a form giving consent for the doctor to deliver their baby. Others were sterilized without even the formality of signing. My fluent knowledge of English saved me.

As a child growing up in Oklahoma, I liked to be told the story of my birth. I begged for it while my mother cleaned and ironed.

"You almost killed me," she would say. "We almost died."

I loved to hear the story of my warrior fight for my breath. The way my mother told the story, I was given only so much time on the ventilator and I had to decide to live. I had been strong. I had been brave.

My parents felt lucky to have insurance, to be able to have their children in the hospital. My father's mother, Naomi Harjo Foster, was a full-blooded Creek. She gave birth to my father in a private hospital in Oklahoma City. My mother and five of her six brothers were born at home, with no medical assistance. The only time a doctor was called was when someone was dying. When she was born, her mother named her Wynema, a Cherokee name my mother says means "Beautiful Woman." She was also named Jewell, for a can of shortening stored in the room where she was born and because she was her father's jewel.

▲   ▲   ▲

The morning of my son's birth, I stirred awake with contractions. I was sticky and hot, tucked in a room the size of a large closet. I woke up the baby's father. I ironed him a shirt before we walked the four blocks to the old W. W. Hastings Indian Hospital. We had no car and no money for a taxi. My husband's only job was working part-time with an older Cherokee artist, Cecil Dick, silk-screening signs for specials at the supermarket. When he worked, he made five dollars a day.

He dropped me off at the hospital before going to work. We didn't bother his mother. She would have to get up soon enough to fix breakfast for her daughter and granddaughter before leaving for her job at the nursing home. My life was poised at the edge of great, precarious change. I felt alone. I had no family with me to acknowledge the birth.

It was still dark as we walked through the cold morning, under oaks that symbolized the stubbornness and endurance of the Cherokee people. They made Tahlequah their capital in the new lands. I looked for handholds in the misty gray sky. I wanted to change everything. I wanted to go back to a place before childhood, before our tribe's removal to Oklahoma.

As I questioned the kind of life I was bringing this child into, I felt the sharp tug of my own birth cord, still connected to my mother. I believe it never pulls away completely. It symbolizes the important warrior road.

Now here I was, becoming a mother, while my mother was a few hours away in Tulsa, cooking breakfast at a factory cafeteria and preparing for the lunch shift as I walked to the hospital to give birth. I wanted her with me; instead, I was far from her house, in the house of a mother-in-law who was using witchcraft to try to get rid of me.

After my son's father left to go to work, I was taken to a room to be prepped for birth. The room was painted government green. It reeked with antiseptic. The hospital was built because of the U.S. government's treaty responsibility to provide health care to Indian people.

Birth is one of the most sacred acts we take part in and witness in our lives. But sacredness appeared to be far from my labor room in the Indian hospital. It was difficult to bear the actuality of it, and to bear it alone. A woman screamed in pain and fear as she labored in the next room. I wanted to comfort her. The nurse used her as a bad example for the rest of us, who were struggling to keep our suffering silent.

The doctor was a military man who had signed on the watch not for the love of healing or in awe of the miracle of birth but to fulfill a contract for medical school payments. I was a statistic to him. He touched me mechanically.

When it was time, I was wheeled to the delivery room. I was given a spinal, which sent fire into my legs. My body instinctively tried to sit up, to get on all fours.

"If you don't stop moving around," warned the nurse, "we're going to use the restraints." She yanked up one of the restraints and shook it.

It is natural to sit or squat to give birth. Lying down forces the body to work harder, against the tremendous flow of muscle and the urge to live.

In the bag of memories that I am carrying into the next world is a living image of my son covered with blood, amniotic fluid, and vernix. He has taken his first breath, and the doctor is stitching me up. The nurse is checking vitals. My son and I stare at each other in the stunning moment of that sacred vow. His eyes are black and knowing. He looks to me with full knowledge of his place in this story. He will soon forget it. I look at him with an unbearable love, and with troubling questions: What have I gotten myself into? How will we ever make it through? I have never felt so vulnerable.

We both slept hard, the weight of chemicals heavy in our bodies. We were exhausted from the journey. When I woke early the next morning, I yearned to hold and nurse my child. I was not allowed to sit up or walk because of the possibility of paralysis (one of the drug's side effects). When I finally got to hold my boy, the nurse stood guard as if I would hurt him. I was young and Indian and therefore ignorant. I bent my mind around her judgment and cradled my son, checking out his perfect little body. I was proud of what my body and spirit had accomplished despite the alienation of giving birth in a hospital.

We left the hospital as soon as possible. My son would flourish on beans and cornbread, and on the dreams and stories we fed him.

▲   ▲   ▲

My mother-in-law blamed me for the fix her son was in. He had returned from his studies in the postgraduate program at Indian school with no job prospects and with yet another pregnant teenage wife who shifted his fortunes. I was the other woman in her life, the reason for his lack of success, for her suffering. I had the one man bound to her by blood and guilt, a sticky bond. Every man she had been with had given her a child, then abandoned her, including her son, who had left her with his daughter while he went to school in the Southwest. I was now in the way, and she took every opportunity to remind me.

She threw nothing away. Every item of clothing that her children had ever worn, every toy they had ever played with, every piece of paper with their names on it, she packed into boxes she piled high in her house, to the ceiling. She would not throw away her son because of a strange, foolish girl.

I wasn't pleased about the situation either. None of this had figured into my map for a life, though I must admit the map was never clearly drawn. My path meandered according to the whim of failed adults and chance. It headed wanly toward the life of a painter, like my Aunt Lois, who traveled from the Creek Nation all over the country without the encumbrance of a husband or children and had the money to buy paint, canvas, and a car. Living as an artist was as close to my now limited universe as the planet Mars. Despite all my attempts at flight, I couldn't afford art supplies, not even a junked car.

Strange things would happen around the house in the dark. One night one of my mother-in-law's enemies came to her as a bird. It sat in a tree outside the living room window. I'll always remember the haunting cry, like the peculiar howl of the dog in my family that always foretold

a death. It sent shivers through all of us. When I heard the
bird calling and calling, I picked up my newly born son
and took his older sister into my arms, while my mother-
in-law sent out her son with a gun. She told him to get
rid of it, that she knew who it was. I hummed to the
children louder and louder. We heard the shot fired into
the tree. The haunting singing abruptly stopped. Shortly
after, my husband, the children, and I moved to Tulsa. My
mother-in-law followed with her daughter and moved in
next door.

▲   ▲   ▲

Each day was predictable. We got up, ate cold pizza for
breakfast, left over from my husband's shift at the restaurant
the night before. I washed the children, cleaned the house,
and he went to work. I worried about money and what
we would do when he lost his job. He would eventually
lose it, as he had lost all the others. The only question was
when. The last time he had walked out on a job we had had
only an industrial-sized box of pancake mix, a gift from
my mother, for meals, to supplement beans and commodity
cheese. My mother was disappointed with my life and did
everything she could to keep from coming to the side of
town I was living in. She had grown up in worse and had
cleaned and cooked her way to decency. My life was now a
mockery of her struggle.

Every night my husband came in from work in a furious
cloud of anger. He told yet another story of how someone
had tried to put one over on him. He had barely managed
to keep from punching out his "skinny white boss," who

was riding him even though the new waitress was the one screwing up the orders. We had nearly starved before he got this job. The baby was nearing eight weeks old, and as I watched my husband open another beer and pace the room, I decided I had better start looking for work. I would wash dishes, dance on tables if I had to, rather than starve the children or myself again.

Some days his mother would come over and we would pool our resources for food. We were bound together for survival. Her mood shifted according to the nature of our predicament. On the good days we would hit the yard sales together. I was her ally as we searched through junk for dishes and clothes. If she was feeling especially hospitable, she would buy me something to wear for under a dollar.

One morning as I was toweling off the children from their bath, my mother-in-law pushed her way roughly into the house, puffing on a cigarette, then blowing smoke into my face. My husband surprised me with the swiftness of his leap between us. He had never taken up for me before when she slid into her enemy mode.

"Mom, get out of here, now!" he warned her.

She stepped back, surprised at the vehemence of his reaction as he slapped the cigarette from her hand, determinedly pushed her out the door, and slammed it behind her. The smoke followed her.

"That cigarette was doctored with curses," he told me. "She's witching you."

One morning as we struggled to put a bag of stuff from a yard sale into the trunk of her car, she showed me a book of spells written in Cherokee that she had acquired during her last trip home. The book was so old the pages were turning to powder. I didn't touch it. She had stolen it from a witch she saw regularly to combat the many enemies she had in the world: the terrible men, the minimum-wage jobs, and the unwanted daughter-in-law.

I didn't get sick or die that day or in the weeks that followed the witching, but neither did our fortunes change. I began to believe that I had dreamed the smoke curse. I pretended it had happened far away from my babies, my house. What I didn't dream was that each day after she blew the curse in my face she began to stoop. Just a little at first, imperceptibly even. Then it became noticeable, how the weight of the smoke bore down on her as it sat on her back, kicking its legs as it rode.

I measured the falling world by my baby's small accomplishments. He could hold his head up, he smiled, or he laughed. Each increment was a promise of change. Not long after the witching incident, his mother and I were allies again, as we were short on food and resources. It was spring. My mother-in-law, the children, and I went walking at dusk toward the rich neighborhood that bordered on our part of town. Most of the flowers were blooming. My stepdaughter was also blooming, outgrowing clothes and shoes that were difficult to afford. We stepped into an alley, attracted by a pile of used furniture and barely worn clothes thrown in a bin for trash pickup. We sifted through, holding things up, chattering about our good fortune, until a child from the huge house spotted us from his immaculate yard and yelled to his parents that Indians were going through their trash. We ran, holding on to our new stuff in our arms, along with the children, until we reached our neighborhood. We laughed after we had made it, and felt rich enough with our new treasures to buy ice cream. I harbored a vague sense of shame at being discovered digging through someone else's trash. I wondered why the residents would rather throw away the useful items than give them to someone who could use them.

Another sign of spring was the posters announcing that the circus was coming to town. We got discount passes from the grocery store. I took the kids and my sister-in-law to the Sunday afternoon show. It was my first venture out in over a year, and I felt expansive. The arena was packed with families, and the city's kids were swirling with snacks, circus toys, and excitement. We sat next to an aisle for easier access to the bathrooms. The girls asked about everything as we waited for the show. They wanted to know what-time-the-show-started-exactly-and-how-long-would-it-be-before-the-show-started-where-were-the-tigers-could-they-have-balloons-if-they-couldn't-have-a-balloon-could-they-ride-the-elephant-and-why-couldn't-we-sit-closer-so-we-could-see-better-and-could-they-go-to-the-bathroom-even-though-they-had-just-been-a-few-minutes-ago. As I answered, I watched people and imagined their lives and how I would paint them, rejuvenated by the smell of popcorn and the change in scenery.

Out of the churning crowds came a slim man in tights and a cape. As he headed up from the ring, people parted to let him by, an incongruous figure in the middle of the flatly ordinary. He stopped next to me and surprised me

by speaking to me. At first I thought he needed directions or had mistaken me for someone else, but he casually
introduced himself as one of the brothers of the featured
trapeze act, the Flying Something-or-Other Brothers. I
felt suddenly awkward and mumbled a response. I didn't
know what I had done to garner his attention. I had forgotten how to speak to anyone but small children and a
husband who was so desperate for youth and fun that he
had taken to riding around and drinking beer with his
high school friends.

This strange man from Italy was the first person who
had talked to me in months, the only one who had asked
me a direct question about my own life. I responded by
talking about my husband. I told the caped performer who
had suddenly befriended me that my husband had been a
dancer who was compared by critics to Rudolf Nureyev
when we performed together in the Indian school troupe.
He had had many offers to join dance companies in the
East but had turned them down. I nervously talked up
his attributes, but I didn't really know where I was going
with any of it. Then I agreed to meet the man after the
performance.

When I look back, I can imagine how I must have
appeared that afternoon—a vulnerable young woman
dressed neatly but poorly, accompanied by an infant and by
children waving their cotton candy clouds.

That afternoon the children and I watched the Flying Brothers swing gracefully from one small platform
to another. I began to consider what it would be like to
fly, like this man beyond fear from Italy, who traveled the

world flying into space, risking his life while the crowd watched in awe. It was then that I became convinced that this was a job my agile husband could learn, as quickly and easily as he had learned to toss and twist pizzas. We could travel together and move into a world much larger than the one that was squeezing us flat, far, far away from his mother.

I don't remember how we got from the circus to the pizzeria where my husband was working the afternoon shift. The sun came in through the colored dark glass in the restaurant as the manager retrieved my husband from the kitchen. I was excited about the possibility of something that might engage him, use his dancer skills, and keep everyone in food and clothes. I introduced the acrobat to my husband. They were civil to each other as I explained my idea. A ripple of tension coursed through all of us. It was my dream of flying, my fantasy. It didn't belong to anyone else.

After I left the pizza parlor that afternoon, the flying man insisted on accompanying me to my apartment and waited as I put the children down for their naps. I was confused about his intentions but offered him coffee, water, and food, which he declined. Then he praised my beauty and asked me to leave with him immediately for Corsica.

The exhilaration of the force of possibility pinned me, for a moment, in the slant of late-afternoon sun. This was what I had been waiting for, but it wouldn't fit, and nothing I could do would make it fit into a map that was apparently there but not there. I told him I couldn't go anywhere, not even Corsica; I had children. I asked him to leave.

The circus left town that afternoon. My husband lost his job at the pizzeria a few weeks later, as I had predicted. We moved to another part of town after he found work in another pizza restaurant, and his mother followed us.

SOUTH

South is the direction of release. Birds migrate south for winter. It is flowers and food growing. It is fire and creativity. It is the tails of two snakes making a spiral, looping over and over, an eternal transformation.

When I lived in Tahlequah I used to walk through town, up and down hills, along the creek, by storefronts filled with items I had no money to buy. I walked when I was hugely pregnant and then after my son was born. It was my time alone. As I walked I could hear my abandoned dreams making a racket in my soul. They urged me out the door or up in the night, so they could speak to me. They wanted form, line, story, and melody and did not understand why I had made this unnecessary detour.

"Think for yourself, girl."

"Your people didn't walk all that way just so you could lay down their dreams."

I wanted more and I didn't know how I would get it.

My days were consumed with the drudgery of survival. I took care of the household, made meals of beans, fried potatoes, and cheap meat. I negotiated with a husband who was essentially a boy. He didn't know how to grow up. His father had abandoned the family and he had no father-map.

There were flashes of inspiration and joy. I saw my son sitting by the screen door making dirt parachutes, his fine baby hair lit by the sun, singing with the radio: "See me. Feel me. Touch me. Heal me . . ." And my stepdaughter in a striped jumper with balloons in honor of her fourth birthday climbing up swings in a park.

But this wasn't enough to sustain the need for artistic expression. I believe that if you do not answer the noise and urgency of your gifts, they will turn on you. Or drag you down with their immense sadness at being abandoned. I felt like I had left my dreams of being an artist in Santa Fe. My husband felt the same way, so we packed up the children and returned.

In Santa Fe we'd get together with our Indian school friends and visit, and while we discussed the state of Indian affairs, tribal aesthetics, and our aspirations at our kitchen tables or studios, we'd paint, draw, and make notes. I made ribbon shirts for extra income, and even tried out for the part of Ophelia in *Hamlet* for the Santa Fe Community Theater, for which I was made understudy.

Otherwise things were the same. Every day my husband went looking for work and came back with nothing. I worked as a carhop and an attendant at a health spa. One day I accompanied my husband to check on a job at a Cerrillos Road gas station. The supervisor came out to the car, looked in past my husband, and told me I was hired, though I wasn't the one who'd come dressed for the job interview. I was wearing jean cutoffs and a T-shirt.

I took the job pumping gas, filling tires, and cleaning windshields. I also made a miniskirt in the oil company's colors, which became my uniform. Lines of cars waited their turn for me to pump gas. The name of the station was changed to Mini-Serve Gas Mart. Months later, when I quit to begin training at the city hospital to be a nursing assistant, the supervisor said I was the best worker he had ever had. After that, he only hired women.

I paid half my paycheck to the babysitter every payday. One day when I was putting the clothes in piles to take to the laundromat, I discovered a love letter from my husband to the babysitter. I'd been paying her to take care of him.

At least she kept the house clean, something he didn't do before I hired her. But the betrayal marked the end. I didn't see it at first, but I was set free. I left him.

Because of my hospital work, I decided to go to the university to study premed. I got help from the Eight Northern Pueblos Talent Search, an educational agency. Without their aid I would never have found my way the fifty miles south to Albuquerque to gain entrance to the University of New Mexico. I was assisted in getting money from my tribe for my studies. I stayed with the Martins, a Hopi family, until I could rent an apartment for my son and me. My stepdaughter stayed with her father. He would not allow me to adopt her.

▲   ▲   ▲

Not long after I began my studies at the university, my stepfather ordered the youngest child, my brother Boyd, out of the house. He wasn't quite fourteen.

It wasn't the first time. When Boyd was around twelve, he was sent to Wyandotte Indian School, near the Kansas border. Unlike me, he didn't look Indian. He took after my mother's Irish side. Nor did he have any connection to the culture. He had been a baby at the time of the divorce. Boyd fled from Indian school with a boy who was teased for being overweight. Both were sent home after they were found walking down the highway, away from the school.

When my mother came home from work, I was told, my brother was waving a knife around, threatening to kill himself. When my stepfather came home, my mother reported the incident to him. He responded by demanding that her son be gone from the house by the time he got home from work the next afternoon.

Boyd was immediately sent to me by bus. I wrote my mother a letter expressing outrage at my brother's banishment. My stepfather was the one who should leave, I said, not the children. He was the problem, I wrote, venting, not our baby brother.

What I didn't know is that when my stepfather walked to the end of the driveway every day to get the mail, he opened everything and read it without my mother's permission, even her private mail. When my mother called to tell me that he'd read the letter and that I was now banned from the house and that my name could no longer be spoken, I reminded her that opening someone else's mail is a federal offense.

Because of the banishment by my stepfather, I was dead to my mother's home for many years.

▲   ▲   ▲

In the country there was a revolution going on. I'd seen it lift its head at Indian school as fresh art began coming through us. Indian country began riding the wave of a giant waking consciousness, inspired by the civil rights movement. We were waking up all over the country, at Alcatraz, in Pine Ridge, in Minneapolis, in Washington, D.C. As students active in the Kiva Club, the university's Indian student organization, we were on fire with the possibility of peace and justice for our peoples. We stepped forth to take care of the spirit of our peoples, in the manner of the Shawnee leader Tecumseh, whose organized front in the early 1800s fought to protect and renew tribal rights and traditions. Our generation was the seventh generation from the Tecumseh and Monahwee generation. Seven marks transformation and change, the shift from one kind of body to the next. Though black America inspired us, Indian peoples were different. Most of us did not want to become full-fledged Americans. We wished to maintain the integrity of our tribal cultures and assert our individual tribal nations. We aspired to be traditional-contemporary twentieth-century warriors, artists, and dreamers.

There was also a revolution of female power emerging. It was subsumed for native women under our tribal struggle, though we certainly had struggles particular to women. I felt the country's heart breaking. It was all breaking inside me.

After one semester as a premed major I immersed myself in art studio classes and dance. I did not have the math and science background to do well in the chemistry and biology classes that were required for premed. I changed my major to studio art.

"I'm not interested in marriage or finding yet another man to break my heart," I remember telling a friend as we stood in the heat in front of the student union. The tech people were making a racket while they set up the microphones and tables for a National Indian Youth Council and Kiva Club press conference. I had just finalized the divorce with my son's father.

A fine-looking contingent from NIYC made its way to the makeshift stage to join our leaders for a press conference. Its members were modern-age warriors in sunglasses and with long black hair. *There is my future,* I remarked to myself as I watched a Pueblo man whose hair was pulled back in a sleek ponytail. I watched his sensitive hands as he balanced his coffee and unclasped his shoulder bag full of papers. He felt familiar, though I didn't know him. I had heard him holding forth at meetings and had seen him in passing on campus.

As we stood in the hot sun listening to the prepared statements, I felt the immense preciousness of each breath. We all mattered — even our small core fighting for justice despite all odds.

That day would become one of those memories that surface in my mind at major transitional points in my life. I feel the sun on my shoulders, hear the scratch of the cheap sound system, and become emotional. I recall a Navajo girl in diapers learning to walk, her arms stretched out to her father. I remember picking up my son at the day care across campus, his bright yellow lunchbox shaped like a school bus swinging as he darted along beside me.

That night there was an impromptu party after the strategy meeting. I watched from the doorway of the kitchen of the student apartment we gathered in, as the eloquent Pueblo man I'd eyed at the press conference easily rolled a cigarette with his hands, pulling me over to him with his eyes. He lit a cigarette and blew smoke in my direction. The lazy lasso hung in the air between us. I passed him a beer and took one for myself.

"Who are you, skinny girl?" he asked. "Come over here."

I pretended to ignore him. He was too sure of himself.

"You must be one of those Oklahoma Indians," he said.

I could tell he was used to getting what he wanted when it came to women. "Come on over here and sit next to me, next to an Indian who is still the real thing."

These local Indians could be shortsighted when it came to the rest of the Indian world. To Indians not from here, he could be Mexican.

"Why would I want to?" I said.

His eyebrows flew up.

"We're full-bloods. We haven't lost our ways."

"And what does that mean? You don't even know me or my people." Then I asked him, "Why do you have a Spanish last name?"

Of course I knew the history, but he had pissed me off. Still, I couldn't help but notice his eyelashes, so long they cast shadows on his cheeks. I stood close enough for his smell to alert my heart.

Then my ride was leaving, and I made my escape.

"Hey, girl," I heard him shout as I shut the door, "I'm going to get you yet."

▲   ▲   ▲

The next morning he called me up and recited poetry. His poetry opened one of the doors in my heart that had been closed since childhood. I agreed to see him, and we began going out. Together we nurtured a common language. I began to understand that poetry did not have to be from England or of an English that was always lonesome for its homeland in Europe. In his poems were his pueblo and his people, our love and the love for justice. The English language was pleased to occupy new forms.

Soon we were a couple living together in an apartment I'd inherited from another Indian student, who was graduating. There was a water line along the apartment walls from spring floods. I made a note to move come next spring.

One night we were out after the bars had closed. I waited on the Central Avenue sidewalk while he disappeared behind the Starlight Motel to take a piss. The vacancy sign flashed on and off. Closing-hour traffic jammed the street. Everyone was heading to the forty-nine, our after-closing-time gatherings in the hills outside the city, to sing our songs of home and love. Cars and pickups passed us with our friends, cases of beer squeezed under their legs.

I looked up at the stars in the clearing sky. Each direction was a world, and each world had its own set of rules, its own hierarchy of gods and demigods, each with its own particular color. I was working on a painting series of tribal leaders, one from each of the four directions, but I was stalled by tension.

When I was five, my mother began standing me on a chair to wash dishes after dinner, because otherwise I couldn't reach the sink. The front of my dress was often soaked when I finished.

"Don't get your dress wet like that," she'd warn me. "It means you'll marry a drunk."

Yet night after night after dinner she would drag my little chair to the sink and my dress would get soaked, no matter how hard I tried to keep from marrying a drunk.

Every morning that I woke up with a hangover after trying to keep up with the poet with whom I was so in love, I'd remember the wet belly of my dress. I'd promise myself I'd let him go. I knew I could not save him, but to let him go felt unbearable.

One morning he mentioned that his brother was coming into town from California and wanted to have dinner before heading out to the pueblo. He asked if I'd like to go to Jack's for pizza with them. I knew that his brother was a hard drinker. I tried to ignore the premonition and remembered his words after the last binge, when he had promised that he was going to quit drinking. Jack's, though it was also a pizza joint, was one of his favorite bars. They did make the best pizza. I decided to go.

That night after cleaning the house for company, I took my son to the babysitter. When I handed him over with his pack of clothes, toys, and snacks, I hugged him close, savoring his freshly shampooed hair.

When my son saw the babysitter's new puppy, he wriggled free to go play with it. The babysitter was roasting green chilies and had just pulled out of the oven a fresh batch of little fruit pies that her people made. She offered me some. I wanted to stay put in her warm house, to wash dishes, set the table, and visit and forget the teeth of anxiety. If I followed it to the source, I would be slammed back into childhood, to my father staggering in drunk and beating my mother.

The first time the poet hit me was on a Saturday night. We hadn't been together long. We were in that amazed state of awe at finding each other in all the millions and billions of people in the world. We were partying at Okie Joe's up the street. He was talking politics with his buddies while I played pool with some of the other native students in the back room. I kept feeding the jukebox quarters, playing the Rolling Stones, "Wild horses couldn't drag me away," over and over again.

He was down about the anniversary of the death of his best friend, who had been his idol. He had been the only man from a pueblo to finish law school at the university, and he fought the U.S. legal system by any means possible, including his fists. But he couldn't fight alcohol. He was taken down by drink, his body found in a field weeks after his death. His grieving brothers were honoring him that night at the bar by drinking themselves to oblivion. They were getting rowdy.

I tried to ignore them and kept shooting the solid balls into the pockets of the pool table, just as I had ignored my father when he and his friends partied, argued, and played. I knew the routine. There was a high, and then there was a low.

Every tiny hair on the back of my neck went on alert when I heard his voice yelling above the crowd, "Fuck you!" We all ran in from the pool tables to see what was the matter. He aimed a pitcher of beer at the bartender; it missed and smashed into the bar mirror with a terrible crash. We all scattered as the bartender called the police. The poet refused to go; instead he decided to climb the fence to the roof of the bar. I tried to stop him. He climbed to the roof and jumped, then stood up, unhurt, like a defiant child, and walked away, the sound of approaching sirens growing loud and shrill.

I should have left him then. Instead I caught a ride back with friends who tried to convince me to leave him.

"No, I want to get the sad goodbye over with," I told them.

They convinced me to stay the night with one of them and go back in the morning. The next day, when I opened the door, all the lights in the house were on, the stereo was playing Kris Kristofferson, "Sunday Morning Coming Down," and all the burners were on full blast, filling the house with gas. He was passed out on the couch with an unlit cigarette and matches in his hands from starting to make breakfast.

Later he apologized profusely. *This will never happen again,* he promised. He made us his specialty breakfast: chorizo and eggs. He came back from the 7-Eleven with a newspaper and a bouquet of wilted flowers. I told him to pack his bags and get out.

"No," he said. "We can't work politically for a better world for the people if we can't hold it together in our own house."

I convinced myself that we owed it to ourselves to keep trying. I found excuses: He had been overcome with grief for his buddy. He was an Indian man in a white world. And most of the time he wasn't like that, I reasoned.

I stayed with him. He planted a garden with my son in the small yard behind the apartment. He wrote beautiful poetry to me. He loved me.

"So did your father," one of my friends reminded me. "You've gone and married your father."

I didn't want to hear it, and felt even more alone in the path I had chosen.

▲   ▲   ▲

That night as we walked home from the bar and I waited for him behind the motel, he seemed to take forever. It was about two-thirty in the morning, and as I stood there the avenue grew quieter after the initial rush of traffic from the bar. The desk lamp inside the motel office made me lonely. I felt far away from everything.

I carried an ache under my ribs that was like radar: it told me I was miles away from the world I intended to make for my son and myself. I saw my easel set up in the corner of the living room in our apartment, next to my son's box of toys. I imagined having the money to walk up to the motel office to rent a room of my own. I knew what I would do: I would sleep until I could sleep no more. I would wake up with my dreams and listen and sketch and paint the visions I had put aside to take care of everyone else.

I recalled the dream I'd had of a daughter who wanted to be born. I had been painting all night when she appeared to me. She was a baby with fat cheeks, and then she was a grown woman. She asked me to give birth to her. *This isn't a good time,* I told her. I was in the middle of finals and assisting in planning for a protest of the killing of Navajo street drunks for fun by some white high school students. They had just been questioned and set free with no punishment. *Why come into this kind of world?* I asked her. Her intent made a fine unwavering line that connected my heart to hers.

I walked behind the motel to look for him. I found his shoes under a tree. Beyond them were his socks, like two dark salamanders. A little farther beyond his socks was his belt, and then I followed a trail of pants, shirt, and underwear until I was standing in the courtyard of the motel. My stomach turned and twisted as I considered all the scenarios a naked, drunk Indian man might get into in a motel on the main street of the city.

I heard a splash in the pool. I remember thinking, *He's a Pueblo Indian; he can't swim.* I considered leaving him there to flounder. It would be his foolish fault, as well as the fault of a society that builds its cities over our holy places. At that moment, his disappearance would be a sudden relief. It was then that I first felt our daughter moving within me. She awakened me with a flutter, a kick. As I walked to the pool, I didn't know whether to laugh or cry.

I never told her father about the night she showed up to announce her intentions, or how I saw her spirit when she was conceived, wavering above us on a fine sheen of light. I never told my daughter how I pulled her father from deep water.

Not long after Rainy Dawn was born on a hot July day in Albuquerque when everyone was wishing for rain.

I can still close my eyes and open them four floors up
looking south and west from the hospital
in the approximate direction of Acoma—
and farther on to the roofs of the houses of the gods who have
    learned
there are no endings, only beginnings.
That day so hot, heat danced in waves off bright car tops, we both
stood poised at that door from the east, listened for a long time
to the sound of our grandmothers' voices
the brushing wind of sacred wings, the rattle of
rain drops in dry gourds.

I had to participate in the dreaming of you into memory,
cupped your head in the bowl of my body
as ancestors lined up to give you a name made of their dreams
    cast once more
into this stew of precious spirit and flesh.
And let you go, as I am letting you go once more in this ceremony
of the living.
And when you were born I held you wet and unfolding,
like a butterfly newly born from the chrysalis of my body.
And breathed with you as you breathed your first breath.
Then was your promise to take it on like the rest of us,
this immense journey, for love, for rain.

▲   ▲   ▲

I felt close to my ancestors when I painted. This is how I came to know my grandmother Naomi Harjo Foster intimately. I never got to know her in person because she died long before I was born.

Throughout childhood I studied her drawing of two horses running in a storm, which lived on the wall of our living room. And now, as an art major at the university, I found her in the long silences, in between the long, meditative breaths that happen when you interact with the soul of creation.

I began to know her within the memory of my hands as they sketched. Bones have consciousness. Within marrow is memory. I heard her soft voice and saw where my father got his sensitive, dreaming eyes. Like her, he did not like the hard edges of earth existence. He drank to soften them. She painted to make a doorway between realms.

As I moved pencil across paper and brush across canvas, my grandmother existed again. She was as present as these words. I saw a woman who liked soft velvets, a clean-cut line. She was often perceived as "strange" because she appeared closer to death than to life. I felt sadness as grief in her lungs. The grief came from the tears of thousands of our tribe when we were uprooted and forced to walk the long miles west to Indian Territory. They were the tears of the dead and the tears of those who remained to bury the dead. We had to keep walking. We were still walking, trying to make it through to home. The tears spoiled in her lungs, became tuberculosis.

She exists in me now, just as I will and already do within my grandchildren. No one ever truly dies. The desires of our hearts make a path. We create legacy with our thoughts and dreams. This legacy either will give those who follow us joy on their road or will give them sorrow.

My grandmother Naomi copied the famed 1838 lithograph of Osceola, her uncle, to make a painting. He stands regal in a stylish turban with ostrich feathers, with a rifle in his hand. She was proud that he and the people never surrendered to the U.S. government. Osceola did not subscribe to the racist politics of blood quantum that were and continue to disappear us as native peoples. He was Seminole, and he acted in that manner.

Just as I felt my grandmother living in me, I feel the legacy and personhood of my warrior grandfathers and grandmothers who refused to surrender to injustice against our peoples.

Because my grandmother's thinking inspired me, I was

sketching an idea for a series of contemporary warriors to present in one of my university art classes. I considered including Dennis Banks, a leader of the American Indian Movement, and Phillip Deere, one of our Mvskoke spiritual and cultural leaders. He was a beloved prophet and a teacher. I considered Ada Deer, the Menominee warrior who fought for tribal recognition for her people after the U.S. government disappeared them.

As I sketched, I considered the notion of *warrior*. In the American mainstream imagination, warriors were always male and military, and when they were Indian warriors they were usually Plains Indian males with headdresses. What of contemporary warriors? And what of the wives, mothers, and daughters whose small daily acts of sacrifice and bravery were usually unrecognized or unrewarded? These acts were just as crucial to the safety and well-being of the people.

There were many others who fought alongside Osceola, and as a true warrior he would have been the first to say so. For the true warriors of the world, fighting is the last resort to solving a conflict. Every effort is made to avoid bloodshed.

I often painted or drew through the night, when most of the world slept and it was easier to walk through the membrane between life and death to bring back memory. I painted to the music of silence. It was here I could hear everything.

▲   ▲   ▲

One early evening I left the university for home after a full day of classes. I began crossing Central Avenue in rush-hour traffic. It was not unusual for me to zigzag my way agilely through exhaust and congestion, my arms full of books and papers, a child in one hand and the other pushing a stroller carrying the baby while vehicles zoomed in both directions. I'd somehow even balance a stretched canvas. I didn't have to think about it. It was a natural dance.

But this time I was alone; the children were already home.

I thought about what I was going to cook for dinner. Was the hamburger meat thawed, and did we have enough potatoes? And what about salad? It would be dark soon. Was my mother doing all right?

Then, without warning, I was gutted by panic. It coiled around me and opened uncountable hungry mouths.

I would die if I continued to stand in the middle of the avenue. I would die if I continued my way through traffic.

As I press the pulse of memory, I tell myself that if I knew exactly the direction the darkness came from and the shape of the clouds forming in the sky when the panic found me, then I might be able to stop it, even now.

If I am going to die, will I explode into millions of pieces? Will I evaporate? Or will I rabbit out into traffic and be run over?

When there was an opening in the traffic, I sprinted across the street. My lungs were panicked butterflies in gale-force winds. I made it to the telephone booth outside Jack's Bar. I hugged myself. I was alive, but, to my dismay, so was the panic. I'd only succeeded in running from one island of panic to the next.

I dug through my pockets for change to call home, to tell my daughter's father that I couldn't make it. I shook as I deposited the coin and dialed.

"Please come and get me," I told him. "I can't make it home."

How could I tell him that to make even one step was incomprehensible? That to make it the several thousand steps to go a mile up the road was beyond incomprehensible? I would die.

"Of course you can make it home."

"Please," I pleaded. "I don't know how."

He told me they were all waiting for me. I was late; he'd already started the potatoes. And then he hung up.

I can hear my voice now as I spoke into the telephone. It was flat, a dry plain. In the distance was the muscle of a whirling black tornado. How could he or anyone know? No one watching this slim young woman with her jacket hugged close would have any idea she was dying.

I had no choice but to try to make it home. I didn't have money for a taxi, or even to call a taxi. I was terrified. I had to reach with my mind to imagine each step. I walked a tightrope over an abyss that whirred with the sound of a thousand bullroarers.

All around me students walked by to classes, to study, to dinner or home. Cars went up and down Central. The sun continued to fall toward the sea, into the west of endings. No one could see the force that wanted to kill me. Nor did anyone know how I had to coax each breath, each swallow. I had to count, so I could live. I had to make it home.

For months I continued to will myself to walk and swallow. Vast holes of panic appeared to open in the atmosphere. Crossing streets was particularly difficult. As I came to a corner, I'd hold on to signs, lampposts, or grip the handle of the baby stroller. Then I'd cross in a blur of fear.

One night I was driving back late from Acomita from visiting friends. Just as I started over the Laguna Pueblo overpass, the panic yanked the steering wheel toward the edge of the bridge. I fought to gain control of the car. Just before I was close to going over, I prayed for help. The panic let go and I was able to pull the car into the driving lane.

I was introduced to a native woman who was a psychic. She helped police find the dead. Two of my concerned friends asked her to read me while she was having coffee in the student union. She agreed. She asked me to open my hands. She looked at my palms. I saw what she was seeing. I saw the wreckage of my life, what no one else could see when they looked at me. I appeared normal, as I took care of my children and went to school.

She warned me, "Be careful. You are in great danger." Then she gently closed my palms.

▲   ▲   ▲

One night when the baby's father was away in California teaching poetry, I felt a small island of peace. The children slept. I painted, listening to the song of the cricket who lived in the corner of the living room, near the front door. The cricket sang about the coming rain. It would be a light, misty rain. It was a day away.

I turned on the television, the story box that changed the story field of the world. The commercial aspect of stories threatens the diversity of the world's stories and manners of telling. The television stands in the altar space of most of the homes in America. It is the authority and the main source of stories for many in the world.

Once when I was a student I had two televisions. In one the picture worked and not the sound. In the other the sound worked and not the picture. Together I had a working set—an Indian television set, I often joked.

That night as I sat in the quiet house alone, I was taken in by a story. I was taken to somewhere in the Pacific; it could have been Indonesia, Malaysia, or New Guinea. I watched as a shaman was called to assist someone in need of healing. There was an exchange between the patient's family and the shaman. He called his helpers. He chanted and sang, and as he sang, the song literally lifted him up into dance. As he danced, he became the poem he was singing. He became an animal. A medicine plant accompanied him. He became a transmitter of healing energy, with poetry, music, and dance.

As I sat there alone in front of the story box, I became the healer, I became the patient, and I became the poem. I became aware of an opening within me. In a fast, narrow crack of perception, I knew this is what I was put here to do: I must become the poem, the music, and the dancer. I would not truly understand how for a long, long time.

This was when I began to write poetry.

EAGLE POEM

To pray, you open your whole self
To sky, to earth, to sun, to moon
To one whole voice that is you.

And know that there is more
That you can't see, can't hear
Can't know, except in moments
Steadily growing
and in languages that aren't always sound
But other circles of motion
Like eagle that Sunday morning
Over Salt River
Circled in blue sky, in wind
Swept our hearts clean with sacred wings
We see you see ourselves
And know that we must take
The utmost care and kindness
In all things
Breathe in knowing we are made of all of this
And breathe, knowing we are truly blessed
because we were born and die soon within a
true circle of motion.
Like eagle, rounding out the morning inside us
We pray that it will be done
In beauty, in beauty

I knew I had to break off from the father of my child. He'd stop drinking, and then his friends and relatives would come by to visit with six-packs and brown paper bags of hard stuff. We'd sit around the table and they would pass a beer or a drink to him, though he'd tell them he had quit.

"Come on, brother," they'd tease and urge him on. "What kind of Indian are you?"

I'd get angry with them.

I'd remind him and his friends that he wasn't drinking. They'd look at me askance. I was a woman, and my tribe wasn't even from here. I was not a real person.

But then he would take one, just one. And he couldn't stop.

At first he burned eloquent. He was funny. He'd sing. He'd read poetry that would break you and put you back together with sunrise. It was hard to believe that this was the same boy who had caused great concern in his family when he reached the age of four and still couldn't speak. One of the tribe's helpers performed a ceremony with fire and loosened his tongue. He joked that they were probably very sorry now.

He would get sad. Then he would get angry.

One night I was forced to leave our house in the middle of the night. I managed to wrap the children in blankets and carry them through the dark to the neighbors'. I remember blood dripping in the white falling snow.

When I began dreaming of killing him with a broken vodka bottle, I knew I had to call an end to it.

▲   ▲   ▲

One night after I had forced him to move out, he came looking for me. He'd been drinking for weeks. I asked my friend and her husband from Acomita to stay with the children and me that night for protection. We locked the doors and windows, visited around the kitchen table while we waited.

He showed up a few hours after the bars closed. We heard his footsteps kick gravel in the yard. He tried the front door handle, then attempted to force it open. He knocked, calling my name softly, familiarly, asking me to let him in. Then he kicked the door, yelling, "I'm going to kill you!"

He walked around to the back. He called out that he was pulling down the telephone wires so we couldn't call the police.

The house went dark. We lost electricity.

He kicked in the back window. The glass shattered and he began attempting to crawl in. He was drunk and awkward. My friend's husband entreated him in their tribal language to stop.

The police came just as he got into the house. I watched, pained and relieved, as they shackled him.

The electric cables crackled with power on the dirt lawn. The police had never seen anything like it. Anyone else would have been killed with all those volts of electricity. He appeared unhurt by the voltage and called out drunkenly to me from the back seat of the police car, "I love you, Joy. I love you."

I did not get him out of jail that time. I did not take him back. My dreams had warned me.

I had taken him back many times, when he showed up freshly showered, smelling sweet, with sorry, charm, and flowers. I understood why women went back to their abusers. The monster wasn't your real husband. He was a bad dream, an alien of sorts who took over the spirit of your beloved one. He entered and left your husband. It was your real love you welcomed back in.

During that period my house became the safe house for

many of my Indian women friends whose husbands and boyfriends were beating them. One night there were three or four of us camped out together. We listened to music, laughed, and cooked dinner. Our children ran around in the yard and played. After the children were put down to sleep, we sat in a circle and told our stories.

One friend's husband had broken her ribs. The last time he had beat her she was in the hospital with her jaw wired together. Because she was hospitalized for so long she lost a semester of credits. Yet he was affectionate. He came to pick her up from school once with their pet goat in the back of the truck. I watched them laughing as they drove away together. She left the circle that night because she got a call from her mother. Her husband had come for the children and she had to protect them from his anger.

There were no safe houses or domestic abuse shelters then, especially for native women. We weren't supposed to be talking about personal difficulties when our peoples were laying down their lives for the cause. We were to put aside all of our domestic problems for the good of our tribal nations and devote our energies to our homes and to justice.

These fathers, boyfriends, and husbands were all men we loved, and were worthy of love. As peoples we had been broken. We were still in the bloody aftermath of a violent takeover of our lands. Within a few generations we had gone from being nearly one hundred percent of the population of this continent to less than one-half of one percent. We were all haunted.

▲   ▲   ▲

After he left I sometimes partied on the weekends. One early morning I realized I was partying into the weekday. The knowing lifted me far above the car in which I was a passenger as we traveled from one bar to another. *This is what your life will look like in a few years if you take this path,* said the knowing.

On one path I saw myself in a never-ending party. I would wake up every morning promising myself to change. *Today will be the day,* I would tell myself, and then I would open up another beer to deaden my knowing.

I took the other path.

Once the world was perfect, and we were happy in
    that world. Then we took it for granted. Discontent
    began a small rumble in the earthly mind.
Then Doubt pushed through with its spiked head.
And once Doubt ruptured the web, all manner of
    demon thoughts jumped through.
We destroyed the world we had been given for inspira-
    tion, for life. Each stone of jealousy, each stone of
    fear, greed, envy, and hatred, put out the light.
No one was without a stone in his or her hand.
There we were, right back where we had started.
We were bumping into each other in the dark.
And now we had no place to live, since we didn't know
    how to live with each other.
Then one of the stumbling ones took pity on another and
    shared her blanket. A spark of kindness made a light.
The light made an opening in the darkness.
Everyone worked together to make a ladder.

A Wind Clan person climbed out first into the next world.
Now, follow them.

Everyone is carrying a light that was given to be shared.

One night after a long, exhausting day of studying for
finals, I lay down and fell into sudden deep sleep. But sleep
didn't last long. I felt demons grab hold of me and tug me
with them into their lower world. I wrestled, struggled,
and fought to get free. I got loose, leaped up, and turned
on the light by the bed. I kept it on all night to keep them
away. They didn't like light. I could see their cold stares at
the edge of the lamp. In the weeks that followed they began
appearing even before I closed my eyes. I didn't know what
to do.

Not long after, some Navajo friends and I had driven
back together from a native rights conference in Oklahoma.
They were crashing at my place before heading back to the
reservation. I woke up my guests with my noisy struggle
with the demons. The next day one of my friends drove me
to get help up near Farmington. A Navajo roadman took
care of me with prayers and the spirit of the peyote plant.
The demons disappeared.

▲   ▲   ▲

Though on the surface I continued as a student who gar-
nered scholarships and made excellent grades and was
now beginning to publish my first poems in the university student magazine, I continued to struggle with panic.
I considered all the possible reasons: the mother-in-law
witching, tribal history, the strangle of jealousy from others, the banishment from my home, faltering into territory

and offending spirits there. But no matter the reasoning, it remained a fact of my life.

I recalled how the dream of the chase began around the time our father left home. It would begin with the sound, just like the panic, like whirring bullroarers making an eerie echo that traveled across time. And I would begin running.

One night after writing my last paper for a class, I struggled in a sweaty, anxiety-ridden sleep. I was running, and then I was cornered in a white room. I could not find my voice. In all the years of the chase, I had never come to this place.

I heard a congested, snuffling breathing. The monster rose up before me. I saw him for the first time. The horror transfixed me. I had no room in my mind for such a being.

I realized how tired I was of the chase, of all the years of the chase.

Just when I was about to give up, the knowing reminded me that I knew how to fly. I thought *fly,* and I leapt to the ceiling of the white room. I felt safe.

Then the monster flew up.

There was nothing else I could do.

With a sudden, unexpected grace, all the fear within me escaped. There was no panic. I was a lightness I had never experienced before in my life.

The monster put his hand to me. It did not touch me. He disappeared. I was free. Free. Free.

I carried that dream back through several layers of consciousness, to where I stood in the future, with a stack of poems and a saxophone in my hands.

That night I wrote this poem. It is one of my first poems.

I release you, my beautiful and terrible
fear. I release you. You were my beloved
and hated twin, but now, I don't know you
as myself. I release you with all the
pain I would know at the death of
my children.

You are not my blood anymore.

I give you back to the soldiers
who burned down my home, beheaded my children,
raped and sodomized my brothers and sisters.
I give you back to those who stole the
food from our plates when we were starving.

I release you, fear, because you hold
these scenes in front of me and I was born
with eyes that can never close.

I release you
I release you
I release you
I release you

I am not afraid to be angry.
I am not afraid to rejoice.
I am not afraid to be black.
I am not afraid to be white.
I am not afraid to be hungry.
I am not afraid to be full.

I am not afraid to be hated.
I am not afraid to be loved.

To be loved, to be loved, fear.

Oh, you have choked me, but I gave you the leash.
You have gutted me, but I gave you the knife.
You have devoured me, but I laid myself across the
    fire.

I take myself back, fear.
You are not my shadow any longer.
I won't hold you in my hands.
You can't live in my eyes, my ears, my voice
my belly, or in my heart my heart
my heart my heart

But come here, fear
I am alive and you are so afraid
of dying.

It was the spirit of poetry who reached out and found
me as I stood there at the doorway between panic and love.
   There are many such doorways in our lives. Some are
small and hidden in the ordinary. Others are gaping and
obvious, like the car wreck we walk away from, meeting
someone and falling in love, or an earthquake followed by
a tsunami. When we walk through them to the other side,
everything changes.
   I had come this far without the elegance of speech. I

didn't have the physical handicap of stuttering, but I could not speak coherently. I stuttered in my mind. I could not express my perception of the sacred.

I could speak everyday language: *Please pass the salt. I would like . . . When are we going . . . I'll meet you there.*

I wanted the intricate and metaphorical language of my ancestors to pass through to my language, my life.

Much like the night I witnessed the healer become a poem in a far-away country (though in spirit nothing is ever far away), the spirit of poetry came to me.

To imagine the spirit of poetry is much like imagining the shape and size of the knowing. It is a kind of resurrection light; it is the tall ancestor spirit who has been with me since the beginning, or a bear or a hummingbird. It is a hundred horses running the land in a soft mist, or it is a woman undressing for her beloved in firelight. It is none of these things. It is more than everything.

"You're coming with me, poor thing. You don't know how to listen. You don't know how to speak. You don't know how to sing. I will teach you."

I followed poetry.

AFTERWORD

The panic followed me for many years. In the beginning it almost took my life. Like a comet hurtling on a journey through a sky path, I lost particles and let go of that which did not support me.

One winter dusk, thirty years later, I paddled an outrigger canoe in deep turquoise waters off the shore of Maunalua Bay on the beloved island of O'ahu in the Hawaiian Islands. I noticed how my thoughts had become like waves, rising and falling without anxiety or urgency to them.

And I realized that I had let go of the remnant tentacles of panic that had been planted in me years ago, when I was a young mother, lost in the middle of traffic. I let it go. I let it go in beauty, with love, in the spirit of *vnvketkv*, aloha or compassion. I let my thoughts of forgiveness for myself and for others in the story follow the waves of the ocean in prayer.

ACKNOWLEDGMENTS

This book is a journey of several years. I thank my editor at Norton, Jill Bialosky, for her faith, belief, and patience.

Two important American writers made this book possible: the storyteller, poet, and artist N. Scott Momaday and the Laguna Pueblo writer, artist, and prophet Leslie Silko.

A 2008 Rasmussen Fellowship from United States Artists, the NEA, and the Barbara Deming Fund provided financial assistance.

For editing and advice with the story along the way: Laura Coltelli, Sharon Oard Warner, Lurline Wailana McGregor, Tanaya Winder, Sarita London, Tony James, John Crawford, William Pitt Root, Pam Uschuk, Candyce Childers, Dennis Mathis, Cynthia Hess, Pam Kingsbury, Gayle Elliott, and Charlie Hill.

For assistance with photographs: Patrick Carr.

With special thanks to my cousin George Coser, Jr., who shares stories with other tribal members and me to ensure that we continue; and to the knowing and my ancestors for their teachings and insights.

I thank my many teachers from the many directions, in all their many forms. Mvto, mvto.

I thank my mother, Wynema Jewell Baker, and my father, Allen W. Foster, Jr., for their part in the story, for their ongoing love, and my brothers, Allen and Boyd, and sister, Margaret, for walking alongside me. I also acknowledge my stepsister, Sandra Aston, for her protection and love.

I am grateful for my children, Ratonia, Phil, and Rainy, for my nieces and nephews, for my beloved grandchildren, and for those who will follow us. You inspire me. May you always find support for your own creative gifts, your insights, and your visions.

I also thank my children's fathers for their part in the story. We have continued to grow in understanding.

May our eyes and ears continue to open to hear and know our ancestors. May we remember the stories. May this story be food for your own.

Prologue, from *The Woman Who Fell from the Sky*, New York: W. W. Norton, 1994.

"This is My Heart," from *A Map to the Next World*, New York: W. W. Norton, 2001.

"Rabbit Is Up to Tricks," from *Wings of Night Sky, Wings of Morning Light*, a play.

"This Morning I Pray for my Enemies," from *Cutthroat* magazine and *Massachusetts Review*, vol. 50, no. 1, p. 232.

"The Flood," from *Stories for a Winter's Night: Short Fiction by Native Americans*, edited by Maurice Kenny, Buffalo: White Pine Press, 1991; *Best of the West 4: New Stories from the Wide Side of Missouri*, ed. James Thomas, New York: W. W. Norton, 1991.

"Rainy Dawn," from *In Mad Love and War*, Middleton: Wesleyan University Press, 1990.

"Eagle Poem," from *In Mad Love and War*, Middleton: Wesleyan University Press, 1990.

"I Give You Back," or "Fear Poem," from *She Had Some Horses*, New York: W. W. Norton, 2008.

"The Flying Man," from *ZYZZYVA* magazine, issue 16.1, spring 2000.

"How to Get to the Planet Venus," from *Sister Nations: Native American Women Writers on Community*, ed. Heidi Erdrich and Laura Tohe, St. Paul: Minnesota Historical Society Press, 2002, pp. 162–76.

"Warrior Road," from *Reinventing the Enemy's Language: Contemporary Native Women's Writings of North America*, New York: W. W. Norton, 1997.

"The Reckoning," from *This Bridge We Call Home*, ed. Gloria E. Anzaldúa and Analouise Keating, New York: Routledge, 2002, pp. 277–84.

"Once the world was perfect and we were happy in that world . . . ," from *Wings of Night Sky, Wings of Morning Light*, a play.

LIST OF PHOTOGRAPHS

When Sun leaves at dusk, it makes a doorway.
We have access to ancestors, to eternity. Breathe
out. Ask for forgiveness. Let all hurts and failures
go. Let them go.